MW00444331

THE STORIES OF MY LIFE

AUTOBIOGRAPHY OF FORMER UNDER-SECRETARY OF US DEPARTMENT OF AGRICULTURE

JOSEPH J. JEN

Fulton Books, Inc.
Meadville, PA

Published by Fulton Books 2021

ISBN 978-1-64952-517-8 (paperback)
ISBN 978-1-64952-663-2 (hardcover)
ISBN 978-1-64952-518-5 (digital)

Printed in the United States of America

PREFACE OF MY STORIES

I am a lucky man. Throughout my life, I met many kind and caring people who gave me meaningful assistance and sound advice. Whenever I was faced with a difficult decision, someone seemed to always show up and provide an extended hand. As a result, I was able to be at several high-profile positions and accomplished several meaningful and useful projects.

The highest position I had was the Under-Secretary of US Department of Agriculture. In fact, I was the first and possibly the only first-generation Chinese American who was born in mainland China and occupied a subcabinet office in the federal government in the US history. Many people had urged me to write my auto-biography, mainly to document that accomplishment.

To me, that accomplishment was significant, but how my character, my life philosophy, and the many years of training and hard work leading to the appointment was even more meaningful for people to know. Also, I disliked traditional biographies that only recorded events in a chronological record. I wanted to turn my biography into stories for a better reading experience for the readers.

My stories were separated into four sections.

The first section was about my youth and student-day activities. My youth was filled with stories, such as when I almost lost my life, and my student days showed how my character and my life philosophy were shaped.

The second section was about how a first-generation immigrant struggling to live in a foreign country and making improvements on himself every step of the way.

The third section was my days in Washington, DC, and how I was able to overcome difficult challenges to accomplish many meaningful projects.

The fourth section was my retirement days, dedicated to work on food safety to benefit the society.

There were two people who influenced and assisted me the most in my life. My mother, Lucia Chang Jen, and my wife, Salina Fond Jen. Without either of them, I would not be writing these stories. For that, I dedicated this book to them.

SECTION 1

MY YOUTH AND STUDENT LIFE

CHAPTER 1
Japanese Bombers

To China, World War II lasted for eight years (1939–1945). During those years, Japanese bombers would make constant raids to both large and small cities in China, all over the map. As a result, tens of thousands of innocent Chinese citizens died from the Japanese aggression. I was born in the year 1939, during the middle years of the war. Japanese bombers would have a major impact on my early life.

At the time of my birth, my father was working as a civil servant for the Nationalist Chinese government. Although he was not an active military person, I was told that he was involved in the transportation of the military food supply of the Nationalist Chinese Army. Because of that, my family moved around to several locations, but the Japanese bombers were always prevalent, no matter where we were.

According to my mother, I was conceived at Guiyang, the capital of the province of Guizhou. Right before my birth, my family had moved to Chongqing, which was considered as the war capital of China during the World War II. Japanese bombers made the city a target every day. To avoid the bombing and for a safe delivery, my mother moved to a small farm village called Beishan, which was not far from the city. I was born on May 8, 1939, based on the Chinese lunar calendar. I was given the nickname Little Beishan to ensure that I remembered where I was born.

The Jen family was from Yixing, a township in the Jiangsu Province, known for the purple sand tea pottery throughout China. The family was one of the largest and the wealthiest in Yixing. We had our own family temple, called Qing-Chon, and thousands of acres of land where we planted crops. I was the eldest male of the twenty-ninth generation of the Jen family. If my immediate family had stayed in Yixing, per old Chinese tradition, I was to assume the family's chief position when the chief of the twenty-eighth generation passed away. I had an elder sister, Jennice, who was two years older than me. During our family's travel to Chongqing, she was sick on the road and was sent back to Shanghai for treatment. She grew up with my grandmother from my mother's side in Shanghai. I did not meet her until 1945, when we returned to Shanghai following the end of World War II.

When my grandmother learned about my nickname, Little Beishan, she grew very annoyed. The name Little Beishan sounded exactly like the phrase "little beggar" in the Shanghai dialect. She feared that everyone would laugh at me if they heard of my nickname. She asked my parents to change it before I was to enroll in school. My mother did so and used the name from her days in Guiyang, remembering a small mountain she often looked out from her window called Jwu-Shan. Thus, Jwu-Shan became my permanent name for life. Later, during my college years, my mother converted to Catholicism. My siblings and I were all baptized, and I was given the Christian name Joseph, since it sounded close to Jwu-Shan. When I immigrated to the United States in 1962, my full name became Joseph Jwu-Shan Jen. Many folks in the US call me Joe Jen. Joe is the short form for Joseph.

I did not remember much of my youth in Chongqing. I did have a brother who was two years younger than me, named Little Yuanling, as he was born in Yuanling, a rural township near Changsha City in Henan Province. Unfortunately, he died when he was barely one year old due to a bacterial infection. If we had lived in Shanghai in peace time, antibiotics could have effectively treated him. But we were living during a war; there was neither good medical care nor antibiotics available. In my mind, the Japanese were responsible for the death of Little Yuanling due to their aggression and bombings.

The second story of my life in relation to Japanese bombers took place when I was four years old. We were living in the suburb of Changsha at the time. The Japanese bombers would fly overhead and regularly drop bombs most nights. We became used to hearing the siren sounding at night. We would get up and run into the bomb shelter behind our house. The shelter was a U-shaped cave in the nearby small hill. Our house was somewhat in the middle of the cave, and we normally used the left-side entrance of the shelter, as it was slightly closer than the right side.

One night, when the siren sounded again, the young soldier who took care of me came to collect me from my bed and guided me out of the door toward the shelter. I remembered that I looked up at the sky and saw two Japanese bombers fly overhead from the right to the left. I started to cry and asked the soldier to go to the right-side entrance instead of the left. My mother yelled at me to stop it. Yet I kept crying and insisted that we go to the right. My grandmother was living with us at the time and told my mother to grant my wishes, so we entered the shelter through the right entrance.

Shortly afterward, we heard the loud noise of a bomb exploding nearby. When we emerged later, it was discovered that a bomb had hit the left-side entrance of the shelter, causing it to collapse and killing everyone on that side of the shelter. We were among the lucky few that survived the Japanese bombers that night. My grandmother told my mother that "Little Beishan saved our family tonight. You should treat him nicely as he will do great things in life."

I did not think my mother listened to my grandmother because she continued to be very hard on me and disciplined me harshly whenever I did something wrong. Looking back, I realized my mother was a great educator. She taught me about right and wrong and installed many old and traditional Chinese cultures and philosophy into me as a child. I benefitted from that for the rest of my life.

The Japanese bombers and the shelter story altered things for me. For the first time, I discovered that I might have some natural instincts. As I grew up, I found that my instincts were more often right than wrong. Some great leaders say that "Leaders are born and cannot be taught." I did not completely agree with that trend of thought. Many leadership skills could be learned, but perhaps, natural instincts might be one thing that could not be taught.

CHAPTER 2
A Little Monk

Due to my father's frequent job changes, we moved around a lot during my youth. Often, I was not able to stay at a school for the whole semester. I often failed tests due to these interruptions. Sometimes I could not go to school at all. In such cases, my mother would find a traditional Chinese literature tutor to come to our house and teach me classical Chinese readings. I was not sure if I had learned much from the *Four Books and Five Classics*. However, the tutors did instill classical Chinese philosophy and Confucianism concepts into my mind, which influenced my life greatly. These philosophical teachings included the concept of hardworking and persistent, being nonaggressive, and waiting for proper moments.

As the eldest male of the twenty-ninth generation of the Jen family, I was very special to my grandmother. She lost her husband when she was young, though she bore five sons and one daughter. She ended up being the master of the Jen family in Yixing for a long period of time. When the Japanese bombings began to take place in Yixing, she came to live with us.

As was the case with most women of her generation, my grandmother was a devoted believer of Buddhism. She frequently visited Buddhist temples and liked to talk to the head monks in order to gain wisdom to help provide direction to my father and our other family members. Because of her, I was taught by monks about the theory of Buddhism, and the teachings influenced my life. The major concepts of Buddhism were to be peaceful and calm in life, to be patient, to be kind to everyone you meet in life, and not to react with anger when dealing with adversary. Buddhism believed deeply in *yuan feng*—two Chinese words that I was not able to translate into English. The closest meaning would be "fate".

My father was major of the City of Hangzhou for a period of time. The city was a place filled with well-known Buddhist temples. The holiest of them all was the temple at the top of the mountain called Song Tian Zhu (Upper Heaven). The head monk was well respected by other monks and the temple's followers. For some reason, although the head monk was relatively old, he did not have a pupil monk that would be his successor. By tradition, his pupil monk needed to follow and learn from him for years before eventually ascending to the head monk position of the temple.

One day in 1948, when I was nine years old, several cousins and I accompanied our grandmother to visit the Upper Heaven Temple and the head monk. My cousins and I were chasing each other around the temple ground and were having a good time. All of a sudden, the head monk called out to me and told me to stand by his side. He looked at me intensely and put his right hand on my forehead. He murmured by himself for a while and turned to my grandmother and said, "This kid has wisdom root."

My grandmother understood what the head monk meant. She cried and said, "You can have any of my grandchildren but not this one. He is the eldest of his generation in the Jen family."

The head monk smiled and said, "A me two fu." It is a chant in Buddhism, and he motioned for me to go away and continue to play with my cousins.

I did not understand what took place at the time. Later, my mother told me that the head monk was interested in me being a little monk and be his pupil. To most believers, this would be a tremendous honor that no one could reject. If I was not the eldest male of my generation or if my grandmother put her belief in Buddhism over the tradition of the Jen family, I probably would have been a little monk and would have lived at the top of the mountain in Hangzhou for the rest of my life.

Apparently, the head monk told my grandmother, "Too bad, he and I just do not have *yuan feng*."

One thing I learned from that experience was that someone else could decide my future when I did not have the decision-making power. As I grew older, I tried to acquire the power to make my own choices. Nevertheless, situations often limited the choices available. Orientals believed in fate and were easy to accept what fate brought to them. In comparison, the Westerners believed they could control their own destiny. This major cultural difference between East and West was quite huge, as they each made their decisions in life.

Nearly six decades later, in 2007, I joined the California Agricultural Leadership (CAL) Program trip to Mongolia to learn about their culture. We had a chance to visit the new head monk of Mongolian Buddhism or the lama of their religion. The new lama was a young man in his twenties who was a shepherd and had recently ascended to his role. As a custom, each member of our group bowed to him and offered a five-dollar or ten-dollar donation on the dish in front of him, as he sat in his lotus posture with his eyes closed. When it was my turn, I bowed and put in my donation and turned away to leave. All of a sudden, the lama opened his eyes and made a sound for me to return to the front seat near him. He put his right hand on my forehead, just like the old head monk in Hangzhou did, and murmured some words. He put his right thumb in his mouth and placed it on my forehead, sighed, and motioned for me to leave. The guest monk followed me outside the room and told me that the lama said that I had the wisdom root and the lama had given me a rare blessing. I felt a chill come up from the back of my spine. In Buddhism, they believed in life transformation. Was this lama transported into a new life from the old head monk in Hangzhou?

The moral of this story was that the Chinese people believe that we need to be honest, peaceful, and kind, and treat everyone we meet in life as an opportunity because of *yuen feng*. This is the very essence of the Chinese philosophy.

CHAPTER 3
Elementary School Dropout

Outside the Japanese bombers and little monk, I had little memory of my youth in mainland China. I only recall that I regularly had to walk what seemed like quite a distance to a private elementary school in Shanghai that was administered by the Catholic nuns. We had English class in the third grade, and I failed the course badly. I also recalled that my uncle Tiger and uncle Paul used to give me rides on their bicycles to a public elementary school in Nanjing. It was called Lawnya Elementary School. Later, I learned that it was the best elementary school in Nanjing even to this date. I greatly enjoyed life for a few months in a big house right next to the famous West Lake in Hangzhou because I did not have to go to school nor did I have a tutor to teach me classical Chinese literature during that time.

In 1949, during the Chinese Civil War between the Nationalist China and the Communist China, we moved from Shanghai to Taiwan. The cannons were firing across the Yangtze River when our ship sailed off the Shanghai coast. I was ten years old at the time and thought it was fun to watch things on the deck. My mother ordered me to go down into the cabin for safety. Later, I learned that ship was the last commercial ship to leave Shanghai before the Communists took over the city. Two days later, we reached the beautiful island of Taiwan, known to the Westerners as Formosa.

We first stayed in a small town outside Taipei called Beitou. It was a resort town known for its hot springs. After a month, my father was named the secretary of financial affairs for the Taiwan Province. We moved to a big Japanese-style house near the president's building in Taipei. After settling down in our new home, I was enrolled in the first semester class of the fifth grade class at a local public school. I was very unhappy because I already finished the first semester of the fifth grade in Shanghai. I was supposed to be enrolled in the second semester of the fifth grade. In Taiwan, children started the first grade at six years old. My elder sister and I were both one year ahead of this system in mainland China.

After one semester, I wanted to try to enter the sixth grade at a private school. They did not take transfer students for the graduating class of the sixth grade. I was allowed to transfer to the first semester of the sixth grade, known as the spring class. Upon completing the spring class, I saw a newspaper advertisement of a new private high school that was recruiting new students. I decided to take their entrance examination and somehow passed it and was allowed to enroll in the seventh grade of the junior high. My mother thought I should finish the sixth grade and stay in the spring class system. I begged my grandmother, who agreed for me to enroll because the principal of the private high school was from Yixing, our home town in mainland China. So I enrolled in the freshman class of this high school despite never finishing sixth grade and never graduated from the elementary school. Later in my life, I often joked about my poor education background that I was an elementary school dropout.

After one year at this private high school, I saw another newspaper advertisement during the summer months that a public school called Chenkong was accepting qualified transfer students. I took the transfer examination and was able to enroll in their sophomore class. Chenkong High School was supposed to be the third-best public high school in Taipei. I almost failed to keep up with my grades in the classes. To this day, I still remember when my mathematics teacher announced to the class who made great improvement in monthly examinations. Other students' grades jumped from 60 percent to 80 percent, but I jumped from 40 percent to 60 percent, with 60 percent being the passing mark.

At that school, I met four other students (Zao Chang, Wenyuan Chen, Liansing Wang, and Peter Hsieh). We formed a small group and sometimes bicycled to a nearby tourist town called Singdian. Along the way, there was a pond which we would jump in to learn how to swim. I did not like to put my head into the water and thus only learned to swim frog style.

After finishing ninth grade and graduating from the junior high, I did well enough in the unified entrance examination for senior high schools and was enrolled in Fuchong, supposedly one of the two best high schools for boy in Taipei. Due to my poor grades, I failed English and biology in the tenth grade. The school notified me that I needed to repeat the tenth grade. My mother was very unhappy with me. However, a few days before the start of the fall semester, the provincial education department announced a new policy that students who failed two major classes but scored above 50 percent could have a chance to take a makeup examination. If the student passed the makeup examination, he or she could return to the original class. My English score was 50, and my biology score was 51, so I was allowed to take the makeup examination. I scored 61 in English and 60 in biology examinations. As a result, I was able to enroll in the eleventh grade.

Due to the makeup examinations, I was one week late to attend the classes. At that time, the seating in the class had already been arranged based on the height of each student, from the shortest to the tallest. I was number 3 in tenth grade because I was quite short. When I returned to the class designated as S40, I was placed at number 50, next to the tallest person, Gao Cheng-Ming, who was at number 49 in the class. T. K. Tung, who became one of my best friends in life, had taken a gap year and reenrolled one day after me and was placed as number 51. Two years later, I finished the twelfth grade and graduated from the school in the bottom half of the class academically.

It was a great thing for me to have been at Fuchong for three years. The school was noted for its free spirit and gave the students more freedom to develop interests outside the regular curriculum. One year, I had to take a makeup examination for music class because I did not know how to sing a particular song. I also had problems with the craft class where we had to use our hands to make things, such as model airplanes or drawings. The best thing, though, was that it had various competitions among the classes of the same grade or among the whole school. It created great unity among the students in the same class. To this day, many of my best friends in life were my S40 classmates at Fuchong.

After high school graduation, the unified entrance examination for the universities were next. The examination would decide which university and major each student could enroll in. Somehow, I decided at that point that I needed to study hard for the examination. In doing so, I developed the habit of blocking everything out of my mind and concentrating solely on the books. For example, I used to put on a long-playing record of classical music on the recorder in my room where I had my bed and study desk. Once I focused on my books, I would not hear the music and my mother's call to eat lunch. By the time I finished with the books, the record player had ended playing and made a terrible *gi-gi* sound.

Much to everyone's surprise, I did well enough at the unified examination to be admitted to the best university in Taiwan, the National Taiwan University (NTU). When filling out the entrance examination form for desirable majors, I wanted to be a Chinese literature major because I had strong background and had been involved in writing articles in newspapers and magazines as a high school student. However, my mother said that all writers in Taiwan were poor and could not make a living. She wanted me to major in engineering or sciences, which could lead to good jobs upon graduation and might provide a chance to go abroad for graduate school education. I decided to try the chemistry-related majors because we had a very good chemistry teacher at Fuchong. Eventually, I enrolled in the Department of Agricultural Chemistry (AC), coded as 4563 by the NTU system. AC was only my third choice. My score was not high enough for my first choice, chemical engineering (CE), and second choice, chemistry. AC was a big class with nearly fifty students. I enjoyed the AC class as I had many chances to make friends, to learn to work with others, to compromise in group activities, and to develop leadership skills.

Much of a person's philosophy was shaped in one's early life. In my case, Confucianism and Buddhism were deeply embedded in my soul. The typical Chinese philosophy of being patient, treating others kindly, being slow in decision-making, and not getting excited easily were the way I ended up living all my life. I guess that I was more Chinese than most other Chinese in my age group. Later, I had the good fortune to learn about the American culture. The American philosophy was more about being aggressive, being quick in decision-making, being emotional, and managing by strict rules. This Eastern and Western philosophy created conflicts in my mind on how to handle the many tasks I would eventually face on a daily basis. Somehow, I was able to take advantage of both philosophies in handling things in life, perhaps even better than if I were only influenced by one philosophy. I needed to thank my native instinct in the decision-making process in my life.

CHAPTER 4
Bridge Games

When I was in the tenth grade, I had the unusual experience of learning how to play the Western card game known as bridge. My uncles Paul and Sandy Chang, who were living with us at the time, enjoyed the game. Uncle Paul, who majored in physics at NTU at the time, had a classmate, Sheen Gung Shan, who also enjoyed the game. The trio needed a fourth player for a bridge game and recruited me to join in. We would play two to three times a week at our house, and I learned to become a good bridge player at a young age.

By the time I reached twelfth grade, Uncle Paul had gone to the US, and Uncle Sandy was a student at Dongwu University in Taipei. In his spare time, he was an editor of a monthly magazine called *Bridge and Chess*. He recruited me to translate a book entitled *How to Play Bridge* from English into Chinese. The translations were published in his magazine in eight segments. The translation gave me the opportunity to further my knowledge of the bridge game rules and playing tactics.

At the same time, I began to play the game with a Fuchong classmate, Frank Huang. We competed in Taipei City bridge tournaments and became a top pair player. After we both entered NTU, we formed a team called Fukuan with four other Fuchong alumni. Despite competing against higher-class players, we almost won the NTU bridge tournament. We lost to the second-ranked team. The second-ranked team cheated by losing to the top-ranked team, which we had beaten. The calculation of points denied us of the championship. That experience taught me that even in playing games, it was not always fair. Strategy and manipulation of the rules could result in unfair competitions.

When I became more interested in dancing during my sophomore year at NTU, Frank went on to pair with his brother, and they became the top bridge pair of Taiwan. Once, they won the silver metal of the Bermuda Cup, the top bridge tournament in the world.

Looking back on my high school years, I recognized that I was not a good student, particularly in mathematics, English, science, and biology. I preferred Chinese literature and had written articles for newspapers and magazines since I was in tenth grade. I thought I wanted to be a writer but did not go down that route. The other thing I recalled vividly was the fact that my mother had an old Chinese tutor who taught me about calligraphy. I used to write big Chinese characters, about a square foot each, using a huge Chinese brush pen. The reason I did so was because if the tutor thought I did a good job, my mother would reward me with some money. Since we did not have allowances as kids, that was the source for me to buy candies.

In reflecting my elementary and high school days, I was really lucky to be able to know folks like Sheen Gung Shan and Frank Huang. Both were geniuses in their own right. Mr. Sheen later became the president of the Taiwan Chinghua University and was also a world-renowned bridge and Go game player. Frank originally majored in foreign language at NTU but switched to applied mathematics when he moved to the US. He went on to become well-known for his high-caliber research and innovative thinking.

A person's high school days usually shaped one's character for life. My high school days were great, and I loved my classmates at Fuchong. Fuchong graduates were more successful in life and enjoyed better careers than graduates of other high schools in Taiwan. From the Chinese tradition, parents only cared about grades, and most of the other schools did not pay attention to the development of students' social skills. That system produced many followers but not leaders. Fuchong was an exception of this tradition. In comparison, I think the US education system could produce more innovators than the Chinese education system. However, the two education systems had their good parts and bad parts. I was lucky to be trained under both systems and used their good parts in my life.

CHAPTER 5
Touring Taiwan on Bicycles

During a break after the unified entrance examinations for colleges in Taiwan and the announcement date, me and my four friends (Zao Chang, Wenyuan Chen, Lianning Wang, and Peter Hsieh) from my junior high school decided that we would tour Taiwan by bicycles. We wanted to take a tour from Taipei to the island's southern end. My mother was enthusiastic about the idea and offered to provide the funds we needed to undertake the journey.

We only had basic single-speed bicycles used for daily rides to and from school and did not have any special gears to carry. In preparation for the trip, we tried to think of everything. We each packed some clothing, a water bottle, toilet items, and some basic medicines. When we were ready, off we went.

The first day of the trip was from Taipei to Xinzhu. We had fun riding along the main Taiwan north-south highway. There were few cars and trucks on the road. Only one of the stretches proved to be difficult for us to negotiate. It was a steep slope which forced us to push the bikes over the hills. Once past the top, the downward ride was very fast, and we had to concentrate on controlling our bikes to avoid a crash. Zhang lost a water bottle stopper, which fell off onto the roadside, and we could not stop to retrieve it. After eight hours on the bike, we arrived at my uncle Huang's home. He lived in a village north of Xinzhu, and he provided us with a good meal, and we each took a bath before sleep soundly till dawn.

The second day featured the longest journey over the entire trip, at over one hundred kilometers. It took us nearly twelve hours to negotiate the distance. We were very tired by the day's end. Our legs were feeling so heavy that they were close to breaking due to the constant mechanical up-and-down motions. Nevertheless, we finally arrived at Taizhong, the provincial capital of Taiwan, and stayed at Chen's uncle's house.

Joseph, wife Salina and son Jeffrey revisited the famous tourist
spots in Taiwan. Photo taken in January 2020.

After such a long day, we were too tired to ride on the third day and chose to rest in Taizhong. We did some shopping to replenish our supplies and had our bikes checked at the shop. We also had two good meals at Taizhong restaurants.

Compared to our last bike ride, the fourth day was very easy. The trip from Taizhong to Charyi took us less than four hours to complete. We were very excited about this stop because we would have a chance to visit the tallest mountain in Taiwan, Arli Mountain, on day five. The mayor of Charyi was a friend of the Chen family, and he arranged for us to stay at the city government guest house.

For me, the fifth day was the highlight of our trip. We boarded a mountain train in the early morning for an eight-hour train ride to reach the midpoint of Arli Mountain. We had not planned on stopping there to visit the mountain people's village but ended up doing so. During the walk to the village, we had to cross a hanging rope bridge between two mountain peaks. The bridge had an iron rope and hardwood panels; some of which were broken and had caused gaps. The bridge was waving in the wind. I was afraid of heights and had a lot of difficulty crossing the bridge even with the assistance of my friends. Finally, we reached the village by late afternoon.

The village was in a festival mood as it was their annual harvest celebration day. The mayor and the village chief exchanged greetings. Someone suggested a friendly game of basketball between the village youths and us. Thus, with the addition of two local police officers to the five of us, we played the game. While the village youths were strong, they were not skilled in shooting the ball. I ended up being my team's center, which was a new role for me. In high school, I was the shooting guard because I was short back then. However, I grew nearly one foot during my senior year and was now close to six feet and considered tall by my friends. In the basketball game with the villagers, the strongest person in the village was their center, who was taller than me. The game was close all the way. My team was leading by two points at the end. Their center got the ball and tried a shot. I jumped up and blocked it. Unfortunately, while we ended up winning the game, I landed on the foot of their center and twisted my right ankle badly. It was very painful. The village folks put some herb medicine around my ankle to help ease my suffering. Nevertheless, I had a limp for several days. Oddly, my misfortune would save me from being badly hurt or from staying in the village for the rest of my life.

Shortly after the game, the villagers started a bonfire and began to drink and dance. The mayor and the chief sat at one side of the fire, and my friends and I stayed closed to the mayor. My ankle was still hurting as I sat uncomfortably near the fire. More people joined the dance, and we saw many young ladies from the village who got up and invited young men to join in the dance. Occasionally, the couple would disappear into the woods for sex. People were singing and dancing happily. The dance steps were very simple. My friends were invited to join in the dance, and they did.

All of a sudden, a big cheer went up as the daughter of the village chief, the prettiest girl of the entire village, stood up. Instead of going to invite a young man, she sat down next to the chief and said something to her father. The chief looked at me and said something to the major. He, in turn, looked at me and said something back to the chief. The daughter's face turned dark, and she went back to her seat. The village's strongest young man went to talk to her, and she just shook her head. Later on, the major told me that the daughter wanted to invite me to dance with her. If I did, I probably would have faced a fight with the strong young man from the village, as it was the tradition for two men to fight for a girl. Most likely, I could have been badly hurt in the fight with the young man from the village. Even worse, if the chief's daughter liked me enough to take me into the woods, I would be retained by the chief as his son-in-law and be made the next chief of the village upon his death. The mayor told them my ankle was injured and that I could not dance with the daughter. I thanked my twisted ankle to no end, though I hardly got any sleep that night.

The next day, the sixth day of our trip, we walked out of the village. I was still limping badly and hesitated at the hanging rope bridge. The strong youth from the village and the chief's daughter came up and carried me over the bridge without much effort. When we got to the other end of the bridge, the daughter placed a kiss on my cheek and ran back to the other side of the bridge, holding hands with the youth from the village and waving goodbye to us. This felt like it came out of a movie or fairy tale, but it did take place in my case.

We boarded the mountain train again and traveled to the top of the mountain. We settled into the only lodge available with five of us in one room, but we were getting used to it by now.

On the seventh day, we were awoken at dawn by a policeman. He handed us some winter clothes and guided us to walk to a place to view the rising of the sun. It was dark, and the road was filled with stones. I limped to the place and sat down. Shortly afterward, the sky showed a line of red-orange color at the edge of the mountain. Slowly, the line got bigger, and eventually, a big orange-colored sun showed its face. When the sun rose off the end of the earth, a strange thing took place. The clouds in the sky all sank down into the valley and became a sea of clouds. This was the first time I saw the many faces within a cloud. With imagination, one could see monkeys, sharks, lions, and other images in it. It was worth the struggle of limping back to the camp lodge. On the way, we saw the biggest living thing on Taiwan, a giant tree. It took seven people to hold hands around the living tree. I asked how old the tree was, and no one seemed to know. My guess was that it had to be hundreds of years old. Later, when I went back to Taiwan in 1970, they told me that thunder burned down and destroyed the tree twice. The tree is no longer there anymore. I guess any living thing will not be there forever.

On day eight, we took the train ride back to the city. The three-day trip was fantastic, and we talked about it for hours and shared it with many friends later.

On the ninth day, we were back on our bike and headed toward Tainan. After a four-hour ride there, we were met by my friend Sun Fuhua. After settling in at the clubhouse of the Taiwan sugar company, Fuhua took us to dinner at the famous Yonglow market. It was the nightclub in Tainan, with many food stalls offering local dishes. The smell of herb medicine donggui was in the air, as the top local dish was donggui duck. We tried some, and the dish was indeed quite good. A couple of my friends enjoyed some fried oysters, though I did not care much about that dish. Then there was a strange dish called "coffin board," which was basically fried breads with a hole in the middle where various kinds of meats, fishes, and vegetables were placed before frying. To me, it tasted okay, except it was very greasy.

The following day, instead of pushing on to Kaohsieh, we stayed in Tainan and chose to bike to the famous An-Ping Fort. According to the fort's history, a Taiwanese general fought back the attacks of Spanish navy three times at the fort. However, the fort was built of clay, and weather had mostly destroyed it over the years. Yet the old cannons were still standing facing toward the ocean. Later, we had the best seafood dinner of our life in which every dish came no more than an hour from the fish boats.

On the eleventh day of our trip, we took a four-hour trip to Kaohsieh, the second-largest city in Taiwan. Kaohsieh was a seaport filled with cargo ships but nothing special to see. Instead of looking around, we went to bed early in anticipation for a return train ride back to Taipei the next day.

Our twelve-day of the trip ended with us boarding a train with our bikes for an eleven-hour journey back to Taipei. After we collected our bikes and left the train, we said goodbye to each other and returned to our own homes.

From my perspective, the trip was interesting. But more importantly, the journey enhanced our friendship, which would last for a lifetime. After college and military service, Chen, Hsieh, and I headed overseas to the US for graduate school education. Chang and Wang stayed in Taiwan. Chang became a high school teacher, and Wang followed his father's footsteps and became a postal worker. We stayed in touch often and tried to meet whenever possible, but we never had a chance for all five of us to be together again.

Eventually, during my college days in Taiwan, I used the bike trip as a topic and wrote a twenty-thousand-word story in Chinese, which was published over six parts in a monthly Catholic magazine that I was helping to edit at the time. Aside from some short stories and assays for Taiwanese newspapers and magazines during my high school and college, it was the only publication I had ever done in Chinese.

CHAPTER 6
Life at NTU

As a freshman of the NTU, I found out that all freshman students were assigned to the freshman Chinese and English classes based on their scores on the unified entrance examination. Thus, I was in the first and best class for the Chinese class and in the last and worst class for the English class. Although I had wanted to be a writer of Chinese stories, I ended up making a living in the US using my English skills. Life was so unpredictable and did not follow one's wishes most of the time.

Although I was an AC major, we had general chemistry and organic chemistry classes with the chemical engineering (CE) and chemistry (CH) major students. Needless to say, those students had better high school chemistry preparations than me and my AC classmates. Thus, we had a hard time, in particular, when it came to the laboratory sessions. I was lucky that for my general chemistry class, I had a laboratory partner who was a student majoring in CE. Therefore, I was mostly a spectator and data recorder, while he did all the laboratory work. We became good friends and kept in touch for many years. I lost contact with him when I went to the US for graduate study. Next to our group were two AC major girls who were nicknamed Old Woo and Horsemeat. Girls must be better suited for laboratory exercises as they were more detail oriented than the boys. I remembered that we followed their lead in many experiments.

Although I did not do well in the courses, I managed to get passing marks for all the courses. The most interesting and the hardest course for me was organic chemistry. A German-trained professor was very hard and difficult to follow in classes. I decided to study hard for the examinations. After the finals, she posted the scores for the class. I got the third-highest score at fifty-nine points out of one hundred. Since sixty points was the passing mark and nearly all the students failed to get that, she decided to adjust the final score of each student with a square root and times ten, up to sixty points. Therefore, all students with scores between thirty-six to sixty points were revised to the passing mark of sixty points. My hard work in studying netted her, giving me one point to pass the course. At that time, it seemed to me that not all hard work paid off. This organic chemistry course gave me a solid foundation and helped me deal with graduate studies in the US. The moral of the story was that hard work always had a benefit, but the timing could be later than current. The class also made me realized that what was the same on the surface could be very different underneath. Although forty-five students all got sixty points for the course, they differed quite a bit in their real scores.

The AC class was designated as class 4563. I was the second to register, and thus, my NTU code was 456302. This was an effective code system. The first two numbers, 45, was the year from the ROC calendar. ROC was established in 1912; thus, 45 represented 1965, the year we entered NTU. The third number, 6, was the code for the College of Agriculture. The fourth number, 3, showed that AC major was the third major in the college. With the right code system, people could easily trace all grades, activities, and other matters related to a specific student.

Once we entered the junior year, I was involved in the student organization called Agricultural Chemistry Society (ACS). I liked being the leader in many ACS activities. One of them was being the editor of the quarterly reports and annual issue of the society. It gave me the chance to interview faculty members and students with special talents. I even interviewed Dr. Ma, the dean of the college. It was an act that no editor in the past had ever dared to do. I liked to try new challenges; thus, I want to be the first editor to interview the dean. I never dreamed that I would become an international journal editor after my retirement. I also did not dream that I would work with Dr. Ma for the development of the Taiwan food industry later.

During my sophomore year, two of my high school classmates, Gregory Chen and Chong Shi Tang, transferred to the AC major. We became the three musketeers of the AC class, as everyone referred us on those days. All students at the AC major of the NTU were required to write a mini-thesis based on actual experimental results during our senior year. All three of us chose the same thesis adviser, Dr. Yuling Chen, a specialist in pesticide chemistry, to do our special projects. Little did I know that years later, Dr. Chen would come to UC Berkeley for his sabbatical leave, and we became friends with his children for life.

Besides the ACS activities, I did not participate in many other social activities at NTU. Part of the reason was that I was younger than most of the students in my class. Thus, I was a little brother to most of my classmates, particularly to the females. I never had a single dating experience during the four years at NTU. In the meanwhile, I was popular to many students at NTU because I hosted many dance parties at my home. There were no clubs or anyplace in Taipei for dance parties at that time. Only private dance parties at private residences were allowed. It happened that we had two rooms, living and dining, which were adjacent to each other, and it had hardwood floors. It was perfect for small dance parties of thirty or so people. My mother liked to have young people around, so she supported the dance parties at our house. Most of the time, I only invited my high school or AC classmates to these gatherings.

One thing that occupied some of my time outside the classrooms was the Catholic church activities. My mother became a Catholic during my sophomore year at NTU. She ordered each of her children to get baptized and pick up an English name. I was called Joseph since the sound of Joseph was close to my Chinese first name, Jwu-Shan. In addition to going to churches on Sundays, I joined a small group of students working for a Catholic father who was a magazine editor. I was also his altar boy at masses and assisted him in editing the monthly magazine called *CheYing*. That was the magazine where I published my high school bicycle story.

Four years went by quickly. I had a fun but otherwise uneventful life at NTU. At the time, all male students at Taiwan had to serve in the military service for eighteen months. The first part of the service was held during the summer between the junior and senior years. It was 1959 when I was in the service at the mountain camp when Taiwan had one of the worst tsunamis in history, known as the August 7 Tsunami. Water covered several villages at the foot of the mountain and even entered into our campground. We were cut off from outside world for several days. Mercifully, no one was seriously hurt at our camp, except we had little to eat and drink for two days.

Joseph's graduation photo from National Taiwan
University in June of 1960 at Taipei, Taiwan

Upon graduation in June 1960, I was made a second lieutenant of the Taiwanese Army. My first duty was to serve as a mathematics teacher at the army reserve school at a little town outside Kaohsieh called Fungshan. I also played basketball as a member of the teachers' team. There was another outstanding basketball player by the name of Kang Tang from Chenkung University. We practiced and played ball games for several months and became good friends. Kang was my best man at my wedding held at Berkeley, California, in 1965.

After the semester ended at the army military school, I was assigned to a unit of the Army that was stationed at Fungshan. During my three months with the unit, we experienced two interesting events. The first was that we were ordered to move to the seashore area to be ready to be airlifted to Cambodia for the Vietnam War. We were ordered to march on foot to the seashore area from Fungshan and stay there for a week. We marched back to the home base without being dispatched. Later, we learned that we were being prepared as a suicide team to Cambodia to support the

Vietnamese War. However, the US and the ROC would not recognize our existence for political reasons. In other words, we were being readied to die and not return to Taiwan.

The second experience was that the president of Taiwan Jiang Zhongchen would sometimes visit his mountain resort located near Fungshan. On one of his visits, they selected thirty-six soldiers among all the ones at Fungshan to be the outpost guard team for the president's resort. Somehow, I was chosen to be the patrol leader for the group. Fortunately for me, they sent an experienced old sergeant as the deputy leader. He assisted me to place the other thirty-four soldiers at various strategic positions along the shoreline of the small mountain of the president's resort. I remembered that we had inspections from several layers of the upper military officers. The last one was the general who was in charge of the personal security of the president. When he found out who I was, he told me that he knew my father well. We did not know when the president was at the resort. We stayed at the spot for seven days with real ammunitions placed under my bed and a red telephone, which was a direct line to the president's office, next to my bed the whole time. If any bad accident took place during that time, I could be court-martialed and be in military jail for a long time.

I was discharged from the Army in October 1961, which was too late for me to try to go to the US for the fall semester of graduate school. Many of my university classmates did go to the US to enter the spring semester of 1962. I became a teaching assistant, equal to a lecturer in the US system, at the AC department of NTU. I worked out of Dr. Chen's laboratory. I was the instructor for the pesticide chemistry and the general biochemistry laboratories. Pesticide chemistry laboratory was a small class, and I had no problem handling it. I did not do well at biochemistry class as an undergraduate and therefore had real problems of handling the general biochemistry laboratory classes. Lucky for me, the regular lecturer who taught the laboratory class was on sabbatical leave at NTU, and he gave me his lecture materials to use. Oftentimes, I had to study hard on the materials the night before lecturing. The students of the class were the junior class of the AC department. I recalled that I had several cuff links for my shirts that were sent to me by my sister and my aunt in the US. I wore them while I wrote notes on the blackboard. Later on, I was told that the female students of the class gave me the nickname Huahua Lecturer, which means "playboy lecturer." Too bad, I never thought about dating any of the girls in the class. Several of them were smart, pretty and seemed to like me.

I enjoyed my life at NTU very much, mainly because I experienced many different things and learned a lot about how to be a leader. I learned how to pursue others to cooperate with me and assist me for different tasks. These abilities were useful in my later life in the US. The Chinese had an old saying that goes "Live and learn all your life." I guess I did that well for my five years at NTU.

CHAPTER 7
First Two Years Living in the US

During my later days of being a teaching assistant at National Taiwan University, I started to apply for admissions and scholarships to US universities and colleges. I was lucky that I received admissions to all ten schools that I applied to, and six of them offered me research assistantships. At the advice of an English tutor, I accepted the offer from the Washington State University (WSU). They offered me the most money as a research assistant at their Dairy Science Department. They provided me with a J-1 visa, which was used for exchange visitors. According to the English tutor, the J-1 visa interview at the American Embassy was much easier to pass than the regular student F-1 visa. Being a poor English student, I took her advice without knowing the restriction of the J-1 visa. It was true that I passed the interview process at the American Embassy with ease.

The other significant thing at the time was that my mother told me to ask my father to finance the airplane fare from Taiwan to the US. I did so in front of my grandmother, and with my grandmother's urging, my father agreed to buy me the airplane ticket. I said to him at the time that I was borrowing the fund from him and that I would repay him later. My father passed away too early before I had a chance to repay him for the airplane ticket. It remained as one of the very few things that I promised but did not do in my life.

My world travel experience started when I made the trip from Taiwan to the US when I was twenty-three years old. I took the overnight Pan American plane to Tokyo, then to Honolulu, to Seattle and then overnight from Seattle to New York. I spent several days in New York visiting the Metropolitan Museum and The Rockettes show at Radio City. Then I flew to Spokane, Washington, took a bus to Pullman, where WSU was located. It took four hours on the bus to negotiate the mountain road. My adviser, Dr. Ashworth, was waiting for me at the bus station. He took me to the graduate student dorm and assisted me to settle in.

I lived in the dorm for the first semester of my graduate student life in the US. It was good, as I had made several American friends. I remembered that one day, a couple of students were in my room talking about things.

Another student came in and asked, "What is cooking?"

I was puzzled as nothing was cooking at the time. They explained to me that it was a colloquial term which means "what is going on." I realized then that I had a lot to learn about the English language. The dorm had a TV room, and I watched TV often. Once when Bob Hope was hosting the Academy Awards show, and he said that Bob Kennedy should get the Best Producer Award. The whole room was laughing except me. Someone finally told me that Bob Kennedy had ten children, and the word *producer* was used as a joke. I began to learn about American humor.

One of the things we did at the dormitory was to play bridge games in the evenings. With my background, I was probably the best player at the dorm. I also participated in the local duplicate bridge matches every week. When placed in the first three places, I would earn fractions of a master point from the American Bridge Association (ABA). One time, one other student invited me to attend a regional tournament held at Spokane. He had a car, and we drove to Spokane. There were more than two hundred tables at the tournament. After two days competition, we placed fourth in the open pair tournament. I got fifty red master points for that round. It seemed that one needed to have three hundred points to be named a Master by the ABA. However, one hundred of the three hundred points must be red points, which could only be earned at the regional or the national tournaments. I did not pursue such honor, as I never had the time to participate in more tournaments in the following years.

All US universities have their mascots and school colors. WSU's mascot was a cougar. The school color was dark red and black. When I first learned about these, I was surprised at how the students were so involved in the games. During the football games, some students would paint their face to look like a cougar or would paint their body with words. They would wear outfits with the school colors. Many students did that, so the student section of the football stadium was a sea of the school colors. I later learned that most Americans were so proud of their alma mater that they would do that for the rest of their lives. They would contribute to the athletic programs of their school all their life so that the school could recruit high-potential players to win games. Many Americans also extended that love of the ball games into their residence city programs. It is an American culture. If an immigrant did not understand the rules of the American football games and did not pick up the spirit, it would be hard for him or her to be a true American.

I had a hard time for the first semester at WSU due to my poor English background. The most important course I took for the first semester was the Principles of Food Processing. When I took the first test, there were four questions. One of the questions centered on how to process a vegetable called radish. I did not know what a radish was. I asked the instructor. He could not believe it and tried to explain to me that the radish was a tuber that was red on the outside and white on the inside. It did not help me much, as I did not know what a tuber was either. Naturally, I failed the test. Later, I went to the supermarket and searched for a radish to learn what it was. As my English improved and I learned more about American life, my grades in the classes improved. At the end of the semester, I got a B for this class. For graduate students, B was the passing mark. I also had a one-credit seminar course where I got a B, as the instructor did not like my presentation in poor English.

The food microbiology class gave me much problem. The technical names of the microbes were long and difficult for me to remember. I also had trouble with the laboratory exercises as we did not have the similar laboratory facilities in Taiwan. I was somewhat lucky to have a girl laboratory partner who majored in microbiology, and she did most of the laboratory exercises. Nevertheless, I failed the laboratory tests. At the end, I got a C for the class, which was a failing mark for a graduate student.

To continue at WSU, I must have a B average for all my courses. Otherwise, I would be disqualified to continue the program and lose my assistantship. The last course I took for the first semester was the biometrics or biological statistics. Fortunately, somehow, I was able to grasp the concept of statistics early in the class. I got an A for the class and was allowed to continue at WSU.

For the second and consequent semesters, I had little problem and got an A in most of the other courses. I even got an A in general biochemistry class. The instructor never gave an A to the student from the College of Agriculture. I also followed instructions well in my research laboratory and worked hard and completed my master's thesis in a timely manner. With the assistance of Dr. Ashworth and my fellow American students, I wrote and published my thesis as a paper in the *Journal of Dairy Science*.

During the second semester, I stayed in the married student housing on campus. Those were World War II leftover bungalows converted into apartment housings. There were not enough married foreign graduate students at the time, so the university allowed two single foreign graduate students to share an apartment. I had an assigned roommate who was an Egyptian. We did our own cooking, although the Egyptian did not know how to cook. Therefore, I did the cooking, and he was supposed to wash the dirty dishes. He did not do a good job of washing, and I often had to wash the dishes again. Later on, I found out that he was from a royal family in Egypt and had never been in the kitchen in his life before coming to the US.

There were only one dozen or so Chinese students at WSU at the time. I organized a Chinese student association. We would get together once a month to make dumplings and other Chinese foods and chat about schooling. We hosted a Lunar New Year party at the student union with songs and dances. We borrowed some custom clothing from the Seattle ROC consulate to show off. It attracted a large crowd. The foreign student adviser attended the event.

In the summer of 1963, I had accumulated enough money to buy a used 1956 Ford Galaxy with a Thunderbird engine. Life became a lot more fun as I could drive to most anywhere. I also moved into a rented house and shared it with four other Chinese students. Two of them were graduate students, and one of them was Francis

Wang, who was from my high school, Fuchong; we were in the same grade but not in the same class. The other was Francis Chang from Canada and two undergraduate students, Nelson from Hong Kong and Ma from Malaysia. We each took turn doing the cooking. I tried to recall the dishes done by our family cook in Taiwan and attempted to duplicate the dishes. Since we lacked many ingredients for Chinese cooking at Pullman, I developed various substitutes with whatever ingredients we were able to find in the local supermarkets. Some of the dishes turned out to be pretty good, and I became a reasonably good chef.

My days at Pullman was a short two years, but it was very important for my life. Not only because I learned much about the English language and the US culture and the American way of life, but also because it was where I met Salina. My adviser was a kind old professor. He was very patient with me and told me how to perform research projects. I learned from him that all research projects have key steps. I needed to pay more attention to the critical points and spend more time on them, a key concept that applied to most anything in life. He also invited me to his home for dinners on holidays like Thanksgiving and Christmas. It gave me the chance to know his son and daughter, who were in college and high school at the time. I learned a lot about American family life and culture from that experience. I had always wanted to go back to visit Pullman and meet with the Ashworth family again. Unfortunately, Dr. Ashworth passed away while I was at Berkeley, and I lost contact with his family. In 2002, when I finally went back to Pullman to receive the Graduate Alumni Achievement Award, I could not locate the Ashworth family. They must have moved away from Pullman.

Joseph received the Graduate Alumni Achievement Award from Washington State University at Pullman, WA, US in April, 2002

Also, I met Tom and Jane Gawronski. Tom was a poultry science major, but we had many courses together. Tom helped me to understand some of the course concepts. They often invited me to their apartment for meals. Jane was a high school English teacher. She would be very patient in teaching me English grammar, sentence structure, and syntax. I believe my English improved a great deal during the two years in Pullam, and it was largely due to Jane's assistance. We kept in touch for many years.

For me to have the wonderful and successful career in my life, I have to thank my wife, Salina Fond Jen, for her patience, friendship, encouragement, and most of all, willingness to sacrifice her own career to stay home all the time and be an unsung hero of our family.

The biggest event of my life took place in Pullman during my last days there.

After I finished my thesis, I decided to stay for the graduation ceremony so I could send photos to my mother as proof that I finished the degree. It happened that Salina came to Pullman to visit her best friend. Her friend was busy preparing for the final examination; thus, she turned to me and asked if I would take care of Salina for her, which I gladly agreed. I drove Salina around nearby cities and introduced her to the local supermarket, and we even went to a drive-in movie. We got along well and decided to keep in touch by mail after leaving Pullman.

When I received the Graduate Alumni Achievement Award, I told all the faculty, staff, and students about the story of how I met Salina in Pullman. I said to them that I thought her best friend was asking me to take care of Salina for a few days. I did not realize that she meant for a lifetime. Everyone laughed. In later years, I met several WSU faculty members, and they told me that they did not remember most of the award winners, but everyone remembered me because of the Salina story.

After graduating from WSU, I was accepted as a research assistant for an old food science professor, Dr. Gordon McKinney, a world expert in natural food colorant at the University of California at Berkeley (Cal). I drove down to Berkley and passed Eugene, Oregon, to visit my junior high classmate, Peter Shieh. At Berkeley, I found my old basketball friend, Kang Tang. We shared an apartment for over a year. Later, when Salina came to Berkeley, she moved in with a college classmate of mine, Tungshan Chen, and his girlfriend, Yolanda, in a rented apartment.

After many letter exchanges, I feel in love with Salina and wanted to see her in Eugene, Oregon, some seven hundred miles away from Berkley. I did not have much time, but one weekend, I drove my Ford Galaxy to Eugene at night. There were few cars on the Interstate Highway I-5. Thus, I was going at eighty miles per hour and only stopped once to add gas on the way. When I reached the mountain region near the Oregon and California border, dense fog settled onto the highway. I could not see more than twenty feet away from my car light. I decided to hug the middle white lane of the four-lane highway and kept the eighty-mile-per-hour speed. Eventually, I reached Salina's apartment in Eugene. Her roommate, an old American lady, was shocked to learn how fast I drove on I-5. I quickly fell asleep. The next day, I drove back to Berkley at a slower speed but kept at seventy miles per hour. When I drove over the Oregon border hills, I saw a police car from the other direction. From the car rear mirror, I saw him stop on the side of the road and turn around to chase me. I stepped on my brake and slowed to thirty miles per hour and kept on watching the police car. When the car showed up in my rear mirror, I started to drive at exactly fifty-five miles per hour, the posted speed limit. He followed me for several miles and finally sounded the siren to have me stop the car on the roadside.

I calmly lowered my window and asked the policeman, "What's wrong?"

In those days, the police car must show evidence of speeding. Since he did not have evidence, he could only say, "I drove by and saw you seem to be too young to drive!"

I showed him my driver's license, which said I was twenty-four years old. He had to let me go without a moving violation ticket.

In many ways, the two years at WSU kind of set the tone for my life in the US in the later years. I was deeply involved in the American way of life due to the environment. Most of my Taiwanese colleagues and friends who lived in big cities were not exposed to this type of American culture. To live in a foreign country and try to get into the inner circle, one had to have the chance to learn about the culture. I was glad that I had the opportunity at WSU. For that reason and for meeting Salina there, WSU remained as my favorite institute in the US.

CHAPTER 8
Famous UC Berkeley

After I settled down in Berkeley in 1964, I found Kang Tang as roommate for one year. On September 4, 1965, Salina and I got married in Newman Hall, a Catholic church that many Chinese and foreign students used because the catholic father was very friendly to us. Some of the other churches were not so kind, and some even refused to let foreign students enter into their churches. Discriminations against foreign and particularly Asian students were quite obvious at that time.

After married, we moved into a second-floor apartment at 1937 Changing Way. The landlords were an older couple lived on the first-floor. They were very kind to us.

Joseph and Salina wedding photo at Berkeley, CA, US on September 4, 1965

The first living experience we had at Berkeley was the free speech movement. Students and non-students staged speeches after speeches on the front steps of the university administration building. National and local TV cameras were permanent features in front of the building. Many of the speakers and bystanders, I believe they were called *hippies*, would jump with their dogs into the fountain in front of the building. Sometimes these folks would stage a protest walk on campus. However, none of these activities affected my graduate student life. The building where I was doing research and where I attended classes were at the southwest corner of the campus, while all these activities took place at the northeast corner of the campus. Once in a while, I would walk to the student union building, which was opposite to the administration building, to have lunch. I would buy my lunch and find a seat near the window. The cafe had ceiling to floor glass window. It was a perfect place to enjoy watching the activities of the protesters without hearing the noises. Salina and I also had gone to lunches on the Telegraph Avenue, which was connected to the campus at the administrative building. We would run into other customers who were dressed in fancy hippie dresses. I think they were called beatniks. I recalled that once, we ran into a family with Dad, Mom, and children all dressed in the same fancy blankets with a hole to stick their heads out. It was quite funny.

My adviser, Dr. McKinney was an old-fashioned Berkeley professor. He was one of three professors in the department of food science and technology at Berkeley campus that did not want to be moved to the Davis campus when the University decided to move all agricultural programs to Davis. The three professors were placed in the nutritional science department till their retirement. Dr. McKinney believed that his students must be better than him in one area of his many specialties to get a PhD degree. This was the spirit for the advancement of science. Since he was the world authority in natural colors and pigments, this requirement was not an easy task to his students. My dissertation research was in chlorophyll chemistry. Eventually, I made some discovery of the photodegradation of chlorophyll that was considered significant enough for me to write my dissertation. I had to learn about quantum chemistry, built a unique gas chromatography, and used manual computers to finish my research work. The work was published in photochemistry and photobiology but was very far from the food science and technology that I had wanted to work in. My degree was in comparative biochemistry, which meant that I had to meet all the requirements of coursework, language tests, and research skills that regular biochemistry PhD students needed to master. The only difference was that my adviser was not a member of the biochemistry department. I recalled that I had to learn to read and translate scientific articles in two foreign languages, French and German. If I were a nutritional science major, I could count Chinese as one of the two language requirements, but not for the biochemistry students. The French was not much of a problem for me, but the German took me a solid six months of hard study to be able to pass the translation examination.

The biochemistry program at Berkeley was very rigorous, and they made me take the general biochemistry course again even though I had taken it at NTU and at WSU. You would think that I should be able to get an easy A for the class, but I did not. I got a B. It showed the students taking the class were of a high caliber. Most of them were taking it for the first time. I did learn from the class and built a solid foundation, which benefited me later in my professional career. The other course that helped me a great deal was the enzyme chemistry and laboratory. I recalled that in order to crystalize an enzyme from scratch, it took me thirty-six hours of work in the laboratory with no sleep to finally complete the assignment. What astonished me was that some students were able to finish it in a few hours. No wonder the Berkeley biochemistry program produced many outstanding biochemists in the world and several Nobel Prize winners in chemistry.

Salina and I lived at Channing Way apartment for five years and had many fond memories. The apartment had two bedrooms and a sizable kitchen and a living room. We hosted friends for meals and played Mahjong games often. The landlady had a color TV, which few families had at the time. They liked young people and would allow us and our friends to watch TV shows on their color TV. The color was more like a paint and was not real colors. I recalled that our favorite show was *Bonanza*.

The research and study program at Berkeley were intensive and put a lot of pressure on me. I developed a severe headache as well as a stomach ulcer. Fortunately, it was detected early, and the ulcer only created a crater on the duodenum wall, and the doctor was able to treat it with medicine instead of surgery. My cousin John Jen had a more severe ulcer and lost lots of blood and had to have surgery in a New York hospital.

The second and third major events of my life took place within nine hours of one another.

Salina was to give birth to Pauline, who was expected to be born on June 8. My PhD oral examination was scheduled for June 1. Pauline, being a competitive girl, wanted to beat me, so she was born one week early. Salina went into labor in the evening of May 31. I took her to the Oakland Kaiser Hospital and waited for several hours. Pauline was born a few minutes after midnight. Having seen Salina in the recovery room, I went back to our house and could not get much sleep. My oral examination was scheduled at nine in the morning, and it took place as scheduled. Four professors, two from the biochemistry department and two from the nutritional sciences department, carried out the examination. I was worried about the biochemistry department faculty as they normally asked the tougher questions to students from outside the biochemistry department. It turned out the opposite in my case. The biochemistry professors did fire some questions first, but I was able to answer them well, so they became silent. The nutritional sciences professors took the opportunity to show me off and kept on asking me all kinds of questions. I did not remember how I was able to answer them. The scheduled two hours examination lasted for three hours. We were finally done at noon. I had a quick bite to eat and headed to Kaiser Hospital, where I discovered that Salina had a major bleeding problem overnight and was still in the intensive care unit. They told me that what took place was that Salina had difficulty giving birth to Pauline, and she lost a lot of blood and thus had to stay in the intensive care for observation. They allowed me to carry Pauline into the intensive care room to see Salina. Salina was happy to see Pauline for the first time. She told me that she had a wild dream that her body flew to the ceiling near the window of the room. Outside, an old man was waving at her to join him to go to heaven. Salina told him that she could not do it because "Joe was waiting for me. He would come soon." I think Salina meant that she needed to return to earth to take care of me and could not go to heaven yet. We think the hospital staff did not take proper care of Salina. The birth was handled by an intern rather than a regular doctor. Some American friends told us later that we could sue the hospital for careless service. We did not know how to pursue it, and I was sure that the hospital record would not show the truth to protect the intern.

Joseph, Salina, and Pauline on Joseph's Ph.D. Graduation
day in June, 1969 at UC Berkeley campus

Near the end of my graduate student days, I started to apply for jobs. The first twenty or so applications resulted in nothing. I realized that I probably needed to sharpen my résumé and learn how to obtain job interviews. I asked my American colleagues to edit my résumé and teach me how to use attractive sentences that fit the job description on my résumé. Therefore, each résumé for each job application had to be tailor-made rather than use a standard set format. After I did that, I started to receive positive responses. I eventually landed six interviews and received five offers. Three of them were postdoc positions: one with NYU at Plattsville, New York, to work on plant biochemistry; one with Newfoundland Memorial University to work on fish biochemistry; and one with the US Department of Agriculture (USDA) fruit and vegetable chemistry laboratory at Pasadena, California, to work on carotenoids. One interesting offer was from a professor at Johns Hopkins University to work on vitamin A metabolism, as vitamin A is structurally similar to carotenoids. The job location was in Bangkok, Thailand. The salary for the research associate would make us live in Bangkok with a maid and a driver. The last offer was for a tenure-track assistant professor position at Clemson University, South Carolina.

After discussing with Salina, we accepted the offer from Clemson University. Besides the position title, the university agreed to assist me in applying for permanent residence to the US. Since I was on a J-1 visa, I could only stay in the US for eighteen months after I completed my PhD degree. After that, I must leave the country for two years before I could apply to reenter into the US. This made the two years' appointment at Bangkok very attractive, as it would fulfill the J-1 visa requirement. I was not sure that Clemson University knew about the J-1 visa requirement. However, they had a secret weapon that I was not aware of. Clemson University lived up to their promise and asked Senator Strom Thurmond, a powerful senator in the US Congress, to be my sponsor. It worked and we were granted the Permanent Residence (PR) status in 1970, one year after I took the job at Clemson. Seven years after we got our PR, we applied for the US citizenship and were granted. Salina and I became bona fide American citizens in 1977.

The day we left California to fly to Greenville, South Carolina, was somewhat sad in the sense that Berkeley was our first home. We left many close friends, and we were heading to an unknown place where we knew not a single person. It was an adventure for us, although it turned out to be a great investment for my life. The moral of the story was that one must not be afraid of stepping out of one's comfort zone and stepping into a new adventure.

Section 2

Struggles of a First-Generation Immigrant

CHAPTER 9
Hatch Projects

When I was first hired at Clemson University (CU), I was appointed as a poultry and meat scientist. Before heading toward Clemson, I went to the USDA Western Regional Research Center (WRRC) to visit Dr. Hans Lineweaver. He developed the famous Lineweaver-Bulk plot of the classical chemical kinetics. He told me about the poultry science field and the direction of current research. Thus, I was reasonably equipped with thoughts of being a future poultry scientist at Clemson. Shortly after I arrived at CU, Professor Lawrence Shewfelt, a fruit and vegetable specialist, passed away. I requested to change my job to a fruit and vegetable specialist and got approved. I not only inherited all the laboratory equipment from Dr. Shewfelt but also an experienced technician named Valerie Paynter who assisted me to quickly establish several research projects. The department of food science hired Dr. James Acton, from the University of George (UGA), as the poultry and meat scientist. They also added Dr. Mike Johnson, from the University of Illinois (UI), as a food microbiologist. The three of us quickly became good friends, and together, we put the CU's name onto the national map of food science and technology in the nation.

It can be said that my experience at CU and my whole life was assisted by the USDA Hatch regional project program. In 1887, Senator William H. Hatch Act created the USDA Hatch project to distribute federal funds to assist the land-grant university's Agricultural Experiment Stations (AES). To perform important regional research projects, one-tenth of the federal Hatch fund allocated to each AES must be used in what was the so-called Hatch regional projects. These projects called for the researchers to meet once a year to report their research findings and discuss cooperation between the AES. At the time I was hired at Clemson, most faculty members were not interested in research. There were two Hatch regional projects; one was on the postharvest of fruits, and one was on the postharvest of vegetables, which both were not assigned to anyone. The food science department head, Woody Williams, asked me if I was interested in it. I accepted the assignments of these two Hatch projects. Each project provided funds to hire a technician, the support of two graduate students, and purchase various laboratory needs. Thus, I had two full-time technicians, four graduate students, some undergraduate students, and research supply funds from these Hatch project allocations. Few new faculty members at any university had such strong financial support without writing long proposals to compete for grant funds at granting agencies and industries.

It turned out that the two Hatch projects were from the Northeast regions. Therefore, the annual meetings were always held at one of the land-grant institutes in the Northeast states of the US. One of the requirements of the Hatch regional project was that the principal investigator of each AES had to report their research findings at the annual meeting. My first meeting was a big shock to me. The entire participating researchers from the other states were well-known senior scientists from their AES. I was the only assistant professor in the group. These seasoned professors all liked me very much because I was like a breath of fresh air to their routine annual meetings. As a result, although my report was inferior to those from the other AESs, the more experienced researchers were very kind to me. They not only pointed out where my research could be improved but also provided me with material and information assistance from their AES. The result was that my research was able to reach the level that could be published in the national journals in a short period of time. They also helped me to get involved in professional societies and nominated me for scientific meeting session chairperson, an honor usually reserved for more seasoned researchers. These Hatch projects not only jump-started my research projects but also gave me the chance to connect with many well-known scientists in the field. No assistant professors at other AES could ever have such opportunity.

At the first vegetable Hatch project meeting, I met Dr. Stephen Chang of Rutgers University (RU), a world-renowned fat and oil expert. He told me that the Taiwan government asked him to form a food industry research and development advisory council composed of Chinese American scientists living in the US. We discussed the matter over the three-day Hatch meeting and came up with nine names to suggest to the Taiwan government. The advisory council was quickly formed, and we met twice a year. At the time, food processing was one of the six key areas of Taiwan's economic development. Export of agricultural and processed food were important to the Taiwan farmers and for gaining foreign exchange fund. I recalled that when I hosted the meeting at Myrtle Beach, South Carolina, the ROC vice premier, Mr. Lee Guoding, came all the way from Taipei to attend the meeting. Besides providing recommendations to the government, one major thing the council did for Taiwan was to hold an international symposium of food science and technology in 1980 at Taipei. It was believed that it was the first scientific international conference ever held in Taiwan.

Besides the council, I was also involved in the biannual conference of the Chinese American Institute of Engineers. Twice, in 1976 and in 1978, I led four food scientists and spent two weeks in Taiwan, visiting the existing food industry and having meetings with high-level government officers, including the premier Mr.

Sun Yunshang. For those conferences, I had the chance to visit ROC president Jiang Gingko and had my picture taken with him.

Our first living experience at Clemson was not a pleasant one. When we left California, it was seventy-five degrees and low humidity. When we arrived at Clemson, it was ninety-five degrees and ninety percent humidity. Pauline was so hot that she asked me, "Daddy, can we go home?"

We first settled in the faculty housing on campus, a converted two-bedroom army camp wooden building. We had to buy a room air conditioner fast to get some relief from the heat. The department head took me to buy a car. I got a good buy without realizing that the car had no air conditioner. We learned that the people of the South were very religious and very patriotic. Southern Baptist was the dominant church in the South. The racial segregation was still fully in force at the time. Whites went to White churches, and Blacks went to Black churches. Even the buses were segregated. The Whites sat in the front, while the Blacks sat in the back even though federal desegregation law had passed in 1962.

To further show this segregation was the fact that when I filled out the personnel form of CU, there was a column to fill in the race. It only had two choices: White and Colored. I asked the department head which one to check since I am an Asian, yellow.

He said, "Oh, no, you are White. The Colored column is for the niggers."

I liked basketball better than football, and CU was a member of the best basketball conference, the Atlantic Coast Conference in the nation. I purchased two season tickets to watch the CU basketball games and got involved in the school spirit. I found that it was essential to truly embrace the school spirit to be a real member of the university. To this date, our whole family still love to watch the CU ball games on TV.

By living thriftily, we accumulated enough fund to buy an old ranch house at the outskirts of the city. To my surprise, the bank that loaded us the fund had a condition in the contract: They had to approve who I sold the house to. I asked the banker about it, and he answered matter-of-factly that "This is a standard clause that we just do not want you to sell it to a nigger." So goes the Deep South in the sixties and seventies.

The folks at CU treated us well. We were guests to them but were not insiders. Most of the friends we made at CU were folks from the Yankeeland or from foreign countries. The one exception who befriend us was Dr. James Halpin. He was the director at-large of USDA/AES. He liked my zest in food science and technology and provided some rare opportunities for me to work with USDA projects. One of them was as a panel member for the development of the Agricultural Research Initiative (ARI) fund. The ARI eventually became the major USDA grant program that funded competitive research through proposals.

Joseph's daughter, Pauline won the gold medal of the Clemson City Elementary and High School piano competition. She was the first elementary student to win the competition at the young age of 11. (Taken at Clemson high school in June of 1979).

Pauline was a bright kid. She learned things fast, and the only way the elementary teacher could keep her in class was to make her the teacher's assistant. She took piano lesson and learned to play my favorite piece, "Fur Elise" within nine months. The piano teacher said that other kids would take three years to learn it. Pauline won the first-place award at the piano competition of the Clemson Elementary and Middle School on the first try. Many people in Clemson knew Salina and me as Pauline's mom and Pauline's dad.

Salina was a lady with a strong will. She was determined to give birth to a son so the boy could carry on the Jen surname into the next generation. We tried hard, but she was not able to get pregnant after Pauline. When we arrived at Clemson, she had a gynecologist at a nearby town called Seneca. The doctor had practiced in Japan for ten years. He did a minor surgery to correct Salina's ovary position. Shortly after, Salina was pregnant. We were not sure what took place, but she came down with a hyperthyroid disease. The doctors advised her the safest treatment was to have an abortion and have a surgical operation to cut down the size of her thyroid gland. Salina refused that and chose to stay pregnant. She had to have radioiodine treatment to reduce the size of the thyroid gland twice. She ended up with hypothyroidism and needed to take medicine the rest of her life. At the time of birth, I took Salina to the Seneca Regional Hospital, the doctor asked Salina that if by a rare chance something happened at birth and the doctor could only save either the baby or the mother, who should he save? Without any hesitation, Salina said, "Save the baby." She was willing to give up her life to give me a boy. Fortunately, the birth was smooth. Thus, Pauline had a brother, and I had a son named Jeffrey.

I developed high blood pressure at Clemson. It was an inherited disease as all my siblings had the same problem. My family doctor was an old-fashioned country doctor. Dr. Hunter treated me with various medicines and kept the blood pressure under control. However, I had to monitor my blood pressure and changed medicine for the rest of my life.

With plenty of research fund on hand, I was busy accumulating research data and started to write papers. My first paper was rejected because it was too long. I separated it into two papers and got published in two journals. Altogether, I published twelve papers in national scientific journals in an eighteen-month period. At one time, all three departmental secretaries were typing papers for me. Shortly after that, I started to receive invitations to be session chairperson of the technical programs of the IFT annual meeting, I attended international symposiums to present papers, and I had food industry consulting opportunities.

I even received an invitation to be interviewed for a faculty position at MIT's Human Nutrition and Food Science Department, probably the best-known program in the field at the time. I did not go to MIT because Salina was being treated by four local doctors near Clemson. It was a good thing that I did not go to MIT. Less than ten years later, the university decided to eliminate the department as it was not in the core missions of the MIT programs.

For the fall semester of 1969, my teaching assignments was human nutrition and elementary biochemistry and laboratory. Besides my visa problem, the other reason that I took the job at CU was that it would give me the chance to improve my weakest skill in my toolbox, my poor English. I figured that by having to teach in English, it should give me the chance to better my English. Having only had one course in human nutrition at WSU, I was having problem in gathering information for the class. Luckily, the department head who last taught the course, passed on his lecture notes to me. With some additional updates, I was able to complete the assignment in good shape. For the elementary biochemistry and laboratory, I had to spend a great deal of time to write up the lectures and create new laboratory exercises. For the laboratory exercise, it was difficult as the laboratory facility at CU was poor. It was hard and very busy five months. The biochemistry department was recently separated from the chemistry department, and they only had three full-time faculty members. I had a joint appointment between the food science department and the biochemistry department.

After the first semester, I decided to revise the elementary biochemistry course from a junior-level course to a sophomore-level course. Part of the reason was to make it so that the premedicine, predental, and nursing students could choose between organic chemistry and elementary biochemistry. Besides using many examples that students could see from their daily lives to explain complicated biochemical mechanisms, I created several special lectures, such as the Cholesterol and Heart Diseases, In-Born Error of Metabolism, and Sickle Cell Anemia. Those were notes I took from the Human Nutrition and Food Chemistry lectures. The results were that students loved the course. It went from 20 students for the first semester to over 150 students in one year. The major headache I had was the laboratory room; it was very small and could only accommodate thirty students per session. It went from one session to five sessions. Fortunately, the university did provide funds for teaching assistants and materials needed for the additional sessions. Within two years, I became one of the most popular instructors at CU. My English had improved noticeably in the process.

Besides teaching classes, I also was involved in being the adviser to the Food Science Student Club, doing extension work, and interacting with local food industry folks. I participated in the Dixie section of the IFT and food science section of the Association of the Southern Agricultural Scientists (ASAS) meetings. Two of my graduate students won the Best Student Paper Awards from ASAS, and one won the second-place award for the national graduate student presentation at IFT annual meeting.

After being at CU for six years, I was eligible for a sabbatical leave for six months with full pay or one year with half pay. I found outside funds to support me and spent seven months at the horticultural research unit of USDA at Beltsville, Maryland, and five months at NTU at Taipei, Taiwan, from July 1974 to June 1975.

The sabbatical leave represented a change of lifestyle and a new experience for life. It turned out to be much more than what I had expected but good.

CHAPTER 10
Sabbatical Leave

After I was at CU for six years, I was eligible to take a sabbatical leave for six months with full salary or for one year with half pay. I decided to take the full year sabbatical leave. I spent seven months at the USDA Beltsville Research Center (BARC) at the Horticultural Crop Research Unit and five months at NTU as a visiting professor at the AC department.

We rented an apartment in Laurel, Maryland. Pauline was able to walk to the elementary school just one block away. My work was quite meaningful because I got the chance to work with one of the top instrument specialists in the country, Karl Norris. We used the lutescent tomato I brought from CU, and Norris built a cell compartment on his huge spectroscopy. We shined light through the lutescent tomato with an ID of four, which was unheard of in those days. The most anyone could get was an ID of one. On top of that, Norris put a red light and a far-red light lamp in the cell compartment. We obtained the spectrum after the light treatments. Norris then used his huge computer to subtract one spectrum over the other, resulting in an action spectrum no more than an ID of 0.01. He then used electronic enhancement to repeat the spectrum one thousand times. The result was an action spectrum that showed the existence of phytochrome inside the tomato. We published an article on *Plant Physiology*. The paper was considered the most significant discovery in plant science for the decade. Needless to say, the paper elevated my scientific status as a good researcher. I also worked with Alley Watada, and we published two papers on the ripening mechanism of tomatoes and peaches. Alley and I attended the Gordon Research Conference in Concord, Vermont. This conference gathered once every four years the top one hundred plant physiologists around the world. I was the youngest scientist in the group. It gave me the chance to network with many of the senior scientists in the field.

Joseph participated in the Gordon Research Conference on Postharvest Physiology held in Meriden, N.H., US on August 16-20, 1982. He was in the middle of the last row.

Two things took place within the first month after we went to Laurel. First, there was a fire that broke out one floor below our apartment. Salina had to grab Jeffrey and run for their lives. Second, I received information that my father was sick with lung cancer. I asked for medical details and checked with my friends working at National Institute of Health (NIH). My friend told me that my father had the oat-cell cancer (later known as the small-cell lung cancer), which had no cure at the time, and my father probably had no more than six months to live. Since I just started my tenure at BRAC, I could only ask for a leave of absence of one week. I was faced with a decision whether to go back to Taiwan to see my father one last time or to attend his funeral after he passed away. I decided to go back as soon as possible. With the help of a friend in San Francisco, who was operating group tours on charter flights to Taiwan, my sister Juliana and I flew back to Taiwan. I visited my father once at his house and accompanied him to two doctor's appointments in the hospitals. The doctors told me that my father could not live longer than two months. He passed away on August 28, 1975, one week after I returned to the US. My brother James and Juliana were in Taiwan and attended the funereal.

The second half of my sabbatical at NTU was a pleasant experience. Our whole family stayed at the NTU overseas scholars housing in Taipei in a single independent house in a gated area near the campus. Pauline was enrolled in the best-known elementary school (ZaiXin) in Taiwan. Jeffrey was less than two years old at the time. We hired a full-time nanny to take care of him. Salina spent time learning Chinese painting from two famous painters in Taipei. She also attended well-known cooking classes in Taiwan.

I was involved in teaching an advanced food chemistry lecture class for graduate students. Although only a dozen graduate students enrolled in the class, the classroom of forty seats was overflow with auditing students from various departments. Years later, I met students who took or audited my class, and they told me that I was a good teacher and that my classes were lively and innovative. Best of all, I tried to induce students to think and to do problem-solving. None of the other classes at NTU did that. Besides teaching the class, I was involved as a committee member of several graduate students and as an adviser to two undergraduate student senior projects.

On my spare time, I learned from an old master who owned a framing shop near the university how to frame Chinese paintings. I brought four different kinds of brushes and rice paper and learned how to put Chinese starch onto the rice paper. I also learned how to measure and cut the mats. Later in life, I would frame many of Salina's paintings so that she was able to have Chinese painting exhibitions at CU and at Michigan State University (MSU). Since I had Chinese calligraphy training from my childhood days, sometimes I would write Chinese poems and put them on Salina's paintings. Many of our close friends have Salina's paintings in their houses.

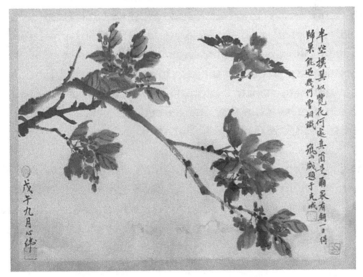

Joseph framed and wrote poem on Salina's painting for Clemson
University Library exhibition in 1977 (taken in December, 1976).

Upon returning to Clemson, I developed a severe allergy problem. Dr. Hunter gave me a test for thirty allergens, and I was allergic to twenty-nine of them. My face was swollen due to a severe reaction, and Dr. Hunter had to give me an epinephrine shot to save my life. I was given desensitizing shots for a year, and the problem was lessened. Nevertheless, I would be settled with the allergy program for the rest of my life.

By 1978, I was quite well-known in the food science and technology field. Besides the *Plant Physiology* paper, I also published a food enzyme paper. It was widely cited as pioneer research in the food enzyme chemistry field. I told my graduate students that one of my secret to success was that I attended a meeting aimed for nutrition, biochemistry, and medical scientists several times. The meetings often presented new analytical techniques that were unique and innovative. I tried to bring those techniques into food science, and I would be the first one to use those techniques. The food enzyme paper was the example.

Besides doing research in the food biochemistry field, I also did some applied research projects. One of them was the dried apple slices in which I used vacuum infusion and low-temperature drying techniques to move sugar into the cells of apple slices. The resulting apple chips were crisp, with a pleasant mouthfeel. Some years later, the products showed up in the market, not only with apples but also with other fruits like bananas and strawberries. My other project was to make tofu from soybeans. To cover the beany flavor of the beans, I added chocolate and fruit flavors into the otherwise traditional tofu. Similar products showed up in the market several years later.

I liked my years of experience at CU and the chance to learn about the Southern culture. With all my success in research and teaching, I still faced discrimination. In general, the assistant professors were promoted to associate professor in four years, and the associate professors were promoted to full professors in another five years. However, in special cases of outstanding performance, early promotion was possible. After I was promoted to associate professor for four years, I applied for the early promotion to full professor but was not granted. However, a White professor, who was appointed the same year as I was but with less credentials, received the early promotion.

One day, I sat in my office and tried to think of what it would be like if I stayed at CU for another twenty years. I would probably still be sitting in the same office, teaching the same courses, directing student research, and presenting and publishing papers. Was that all there was in my life? The thought of leaving started to brew in my mind.

CHAPTER 11
Life at MSU

With the thought of possibly leaving Clemson, I started to check out food industry opportunities and tried to find out more about the so-called real world. The industry folks generally viewed the academic person as nerds. They felt that the academics performed research that were not applicable in the real world. I started to send out inquiries to food industries for possible jobs. Nothing happened for a while. Finally, in early 1979, I got a call that the Hunt-Wesson company would hire me as a research chemist at their Anaheim, California, location. I was very excited and started to think of moving to Anaheim. Fate had it that within two hours, I got another call from MSU. The department head of the food science and human nutrition department offered me a tenured faculty position. At that time, MSU had the largest and the best academic food science and nutrition program in the country. Having been in a small pond at CU, I just could not resist the temptation to join a big ocean like MSU. Salina was also worried about the cost of living at Anaheim, and that we might not be able to afford to live there. The MSU offer matched the offer from Hunt-Wesson in terms of dollar amount. East Lansing was more expensive than Clemson but much less than Anaheim, California. We made the decision to move to the cold Midwest. This was my first career change.

Thinking back on the nine years we spent at Clemson, I learned a tremendous lot about American culture and social justice. I was so lucky that I was able to establish myself independently by myself in the food science field as one of the upcoming young stars. I had to work hard. Salina had to work hard for the nine years.

The stay at MSU did not turn out to be as rosy as I thought. Large institute politics overshadowed the advantage of having many senior faculty members. Competitions for grant funds and publication pressures were so keen that oftentimes the graduate students of the adjacent research laboratories did not talk to each other. The nice cooperative spirit I experienced at CU did not exist at MSU. I realized that the reason was simple. I was the star faculty at CU, while I was a nobody in comparison with the many other seasoned and well-known faculty members of MSU.

One of the pleasant memories at MSU was the high-caliber graduate students. Many students took my courses in food enzymology and advanced food biochemistry as these courses were new and never been offered before. Years later, I would meet someone who would come up to me and tell me that they took my courses at MSU and felt they benefited a lot from my courses. They said that I not only taught the scientific facts but also incorporated life philosophy and innovative spirit in my lectures. They might not remember all the scientific facts, but they all remembered the life philosophy.

Life at the north country was hard living. During the wintertime, snow and ice were abundant, even though they told us that it was a comparatively warm winter. The ground was frozen to three feet deep. When Pauline walked to the middle school half a mile away, the snow covered her knees. Twice, on the road, I nearly had a car accident due to the ice on the road, and I lost control of the wheels. Fortunately, there was no cars nearby, and I regained control before oncoming traffic started to approach me.

Pauline did not enjoy her classes as she did not know anyone in her classes at her middle school. Nevertheless, her competitive spirit still existed. One day, she came home with a second-place trophy for ping-pong tournament. I asked her what happened. She said that only three students entered the competition from the whole school.

With the winter months at home, I framed a lot of Salina's paintings. In the early spring of 1980, she had a personal exhibition of her paintings at the library of MSU. It kept us busy for several weeks.

Joseph framed and wrote poem on Salina's plum flower painting for Michigan State University Library's exhibition in 1980. (Taken in December, 1979).

After the exhibition, we invited the Food Science department head and a Japanese faculty member to our house for coffee. They mentioned about the exhibition, so we took them to our basement to view Salina's paintings that had not been framed. The Japanese faculty spotted a plum flower painting. Salina agreed to sale it to him at a discount. He was very happy.

I continued to serve on the advisory council of food industry research and development for Taiwan and traveled to Taiwan several times. In the meanwhile, food industry offers continued to come my way, and I continued to turn them down. One time, I referred my former graduate student to them. He took the job from the Nestlé tea farm located in Charleston, South Carolina. He had good industry experience and later returned to CU as a professor and retired there.

Finally, when Campbell Soup Company called and offered me a position as a manager instead of a scientist, I knew that it was my last chance to join the food industry. Since life in Michigan was harsh, and I nearly had a car accidence twice, Salina was in favor of moving to New Jersey. Thus, in July 1980, I accepted the offer from Campbell and joined the food industry. This was my second career change.

Although our experience at MSU was short, it did give me a chance to learn about the Midwest American culture. In some ways, that culture was similar to the Chinese culture. People were friendly and helpful to each other, with a farmer's attitude. They were patient and enjoyed friends and gatherings at home due to the cold weather. They were not keen on politics but did re-elected their congressional representatives. Many Midwest senators were senior members of the U.S. Congress and occupied key committee chair positions. They normally did not participate in political election except when they were seeking for changes. That was probably why Donald Trump got elected as the US president as he awakened the sleeping silent voters of the Midwest.

CHAPTER 12
Campbell Soup Experience

In September 1980, I drove one of our cars from Michigan to New Jersey by myself. Salina and the kids stayed in Michigan to sell our house. Once every other week, Campbell would send me back to Michigan for the weekend to be with my family.

Without a permanent housing, Campbell paid me to stay in a motel in Cherry Hill and commute to work. One day, I went back after work and saw a fire-engine truck at my motel entrance. Apparently, the motel had a fire and half of the rooms were destroyed. Although my room was not destroyed, the smoke had damaged all my clothing. I went to a different motel for the night and continued to work without interruption.

We decided to move the family to New Jersey in December 1980 and rented a house while we waited for our new house in Cherry Hill to be built. Our Michigan house was eventually sold, and Campbell paid for the sales commission, the packing, and the moving of all furniture, our other car, and other goods to New Jersey.

As the new manager of the newly formed fundamental research group, I managed only one senior researcher with a doctoral degree, another research chemist with a master's degree, and an administrative assistant. The regular Research and Development (R&D) staff and the engineering staff did not take me seriously. One project I worked on was to find a method to extend the shelf life of fresh mushrooms. I learned about the growing of mushroom in the dark houses or in caves filled with horse manures. I learned to use sharp knives to harvest the mushrooms from the stacked growing beds in these houses. The staff was surprised about my ability to learn these things. I told them about Cal Poly's learn-by-doing philosophy and practice. They were impressed.

To attempt to extend the shelf life of the fresh mushrooms, I designed an experiment using a spraying agent on them at the packing house. The mushrooms were transported by refrigerated trucks to a nearby storage places to examine the shelf life. The harvesting crews at the packing plants were unionized, and the union officers were worried that my experiment might result in the reduction of the harvesting crew. So they went in the storage place and sabotaged the samples. Fortunately, I had duplicate samples and used two separate storage locations. The Campbell staff was not happy with my research design and thought it was a waste of time and energy to have duplicate samples. Because of the duplicate samples, we were able to get good research results from the experiment and showed that the spray agents could extend the shelf life of the fresh mushrooms. Ever since that, the R&D staff took me seriously and did listen to my ideas at the group meetings.

The surprising thing to me was that when we presented the results to the business manager of the fresh produce products, he said, "Why do you want to extend the shelf life of the fresh mushrooms? We want the market and consumers to throw away some mushrooms so they can buy more from us. If the mushrooms have longer shelf life, consumers can keep them longer and would buy less from us." That was the end of the project.

Shortly after that, I was able to hire three more research scientists for my group and had approval for several new research projects. Gaining confidence of the Campbell staff and management, I was quickly involved in other company businesses. I participated in the evaluation of buying potential fresh produce companies and the development of ingredient-sourcing projects. One of the projects was to try to find sources of fresh mushrooms, chickens, and tomatoes in China. I made two trips to China. The first time was with the Vice President (VP) of agricultural production unit and a brokerage agent who was hired by the VP to work in China. When we visited a town that was targeted as a potential site of our project, the locals asked the brokerage agent where was his family. It seemed that they had a misunderstanding that the agent would bring his family and spend a whole growing season at the town. I helped to explain the misunderstanding and saved the agent from staying in that town. We then took the railroad trains from Beijing to Shanghai. The ride was eighteen hours, and it had sleeping cabins. We got to view the vast countryside and agricultural land of coastal China.

The second time, I took the Campbell VP of R&D and the VP of Purchasing to the same and more places in China. I recalled that we visited the mushroom research center near Nanjing, and they hosted us for a mushroom dinner. There were over thirty dishes all made from various types of edible mushrooms. The end result of the trip was that Campbell decided to establish several small experimental farms in China at various strategic locations. These farms were involved in growing and processing the processing type tomatoes and poultry houses for laying hens.

On the way back to the US, the VP of R&D asked me, "Joe, you are a texture specialist. The ragù spaghetti sauce on the market is so watery. Can you do something about it?"

I said, "Sure, I will design an experiment to check it out."

Six weeks later, I presented my results to the VP. He immediately ordered the R&D manager of manufacturing to work with me on producing a new spaghetti sauce which was named Prego. Prego was very successful that it captured one-third of the spaghetti sauce market in the first month of production. It was selected by the Harvard Business School as a successful case study of new product development.

In 1989, I was promoted to the position of corporate director of R&D and was the supervisor of over seventy R&D researchers. Besides fundamental science, I had dairy science, cereal science, and fats and oil groups reporting to me. I was the first foreign-born corporate director in the company's history. I guess that was the first time that I broke a glass ceiling.

Besides Prego and mushrooms, I also worked on V8 juice, cheese flavor for Pepperidge Farm's Goldfish crackers, TV dinners for Swanson, bean sprout growing, and instant noodles development. One of the most memorable projects to me was the Flavor Saver, a genetically modified tomato. There were two kinds of tomatoes: fresh market tomatoes and processing tomatoes. When Campbell went to China to search for ingredient sources, we were interested in processing tomatoes. Processing tomatoes could be left in the field till fully ripe to harvest and transported to the factory to make tomato pastes. The fresh produce business managers had a different tomato problem. If the farmers let the tomatoes ripe and turn red in the field, the harvested tomatoes were soft and would be crushed during transportation. If the farmers harvested the tomatoes while they were not ripe and still green, the tomatoes would not develop tomato flavors. My project was to try to find a way to let the tomatoes continue to ripe in the field to develop the proper flavor yet somehow stop the texture-softening process. The tomato texture-softening process was controlled by several enzymes. The two key enzymes were the pectin esterase (PE) and the polygalacturonase (PG). They control the degradation of pectin, the main substance that acts as a glue to keep the cell walls together. The scientists in my groups did not have the expertise to work on the project. Another division of Campbell dealing with plant sciences was supposed to have scientists who could work on it. Unfortunately, the division head left Campbell and took his group staff to form a new private company. I was able to connect with them and gave them a grant to work on the project. They worked on it for two years and were unsuccessful. So I searched for a new group and found a plant biotechnology company called Calgene, located near Davis, California. With the grant that I gave them, one of the scientists at Calgene found an anti-PG gene in a bacterium and was able to transfer it into the tomato fruit. It meant that the tomato could ripen in the field yet the texture would not soften. Small field tests were conducted and yielded good results. It was the first Genetically Modified Organisms (GMO) plant successfully tested in the field. We named it Flavor Saver tomatoes. A California farmer adopted the technology and planted it on a commercial scale. Unfortunately, the yield of Flavor Saver tomato was less than that of the traditional variety tomatoes. I left Campbell, and the project was terminated and did not continue to seek yield improvement for a viable commercial tomato variety.

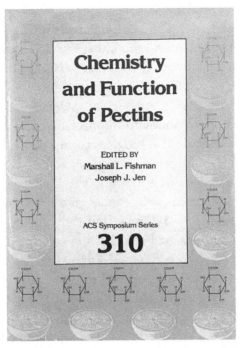

The first book published by Joseph as American Chemical Society Symposium
Series number 310. (taken in April of 1985 at Miami Beach, Florida, US.)

Pauline had a fantastic time at Cherry Hill. She attended the Cherry Hill High
East, which was possibly the best public high school in the country. Besides having
all the regular Advanced Placement (AP) classes, they also offered AP classes equal to
college sophomore classes. Their idea was that their best students could finish the college sophomore classes, and they only needed two years to complete a college degree.
Pauline was one of those students. I recalled that she had a cell physiology class where
she asked me questions that I was not able to answer. She was also involved in many
other activities in school and taking piano lessons and deliver newspapers. Her schedule was so busy that Salina had a hard time driving her to all the events.

She entered the America's Junior Miss competition. Since she did not have an
evening grown, she borrowed one from her friends to enter the school and county
contests and won both competitions. It was then she told us about it. We purchased
an evening grown for her to compete at the New Jersey state final, and she won. So
she became the official 1984 Junior Miss New Jersey. She missed her high-school
graduation to attend the national final held at Mobile, Alabama. Our whole family went to Mobile to give her support. She did not win the national competition,
which was televised on national television, although she did make it into the final
ten contestants. As Junior Miss New Jersey, she was involved in many functions and
gave many presentations across the state. The one that impressed me the most was

that she gave a speech at the New Jersey state assembly. Not too many high-school kids had that kind of experience. She continued to be involved in the event till today.

Jeffrey attended the elementary school that was down the road at the other end of our subdivision. Salina volunteered as a library assistant there for six years. Jeffrey did attend one semester of middle school before we moved to Georgia.

During my Campbell days, I attended an Master of Business Administration (MBA) program offered by the Southern Illinois University at Edwardsville (SIUE). Campbell funded the cost. The MBA program consisted of twenty graduate business courses. The courses were conducted at nearby air force bases and taught by regular SIUE business faculty members who flew into the air force bases. Each course took six weeks. The faculty first taught twenty hours on the first weekend with four hours on Friday night, eight hours on Saturday, and eight hours on Sunday. After three weeks, the second weekend repeated the teaching and ended with a final examination. The program was setup to educate air force managers. There was not enough military enrollment, so the air force opened up for civilians to participate. It cost $1,000 for each course. Without Campbell's support, I could not afford to complete the MBA degree. It also helped that we had two air force bases near our house. Nevertheless, it meant I was out of the house many weekends. Since most of the civilian students were middle and upper managers of various industries, the classes were conducted at a higher level than the regular classes on SIUE campus. After four years, I finally got my MBA degree and learned about many different industries besides food companies.

Shortly after I got my MBA degree, one day, the VP of R&D called me to his office and took me to see the executive VP. The executive VP asked me, "I heard that you have done well in R&D, and you have recently got an MBA, how would you like to come and work for me?" I was surprised and must look puzzled. The VP of R&D said, "We are interested in developing the market in China and Southeast Asia. Would you be interested in being the person to handle that?" The executive VP added, "You can name your position, your salary, and working budget."

I was so astonished that all I could say was "Thank you. Do you think I can handle the job?"

He said, "You know the language and the Chinese culture better than anyone in our company. I think you can handle it." Sensing my hesitation, the VP of R&D said, "Joe, just take the job for two years. If you do not like the job, you can come back to R&D and have your old job back!"

I asked if I could talk it over with my wife. They said, "Sure."

Salina was very much concerned that the schooling of our children would be a problem if we moved to China. China did not have any international schools in those days.

I told the VP of R&D that, and he said, "You can live in Hong Kong, where there is an international school for your kids. However, you have to spend two weeks of the month in China, one week in other parts of Southeast Asia, and one week back to New Jersey to report your progress and receive instructions."

After much thought, my wife and I decided that we could not accept the offer and declined it. I knew that my days at Campbell would be numbered. No one in Campbell said no to the executive VP.

God must be looking after me. As I was pondering how to leave Campbell, I got a phone call from the dean of agriculture at UGA. He said that I was nominated for the position as the division chair of food science and technology. After a discussion with Salina, we decided to take on the offer and became a candidate of the position. After a lengthy interview process, I was appointed as the division chair. It marked my move from the food industry back to academia. However, this time, it was not as a professor but as an academic manager. This was my third move in my career.

The three types of jobs—professor, food industry manager, and academic manager—were very different from each other. Experiences and reputations gained in one job did not transfer to another. Essentially, I had to reestablish myself from the ground level up. It took a while to do so. Maybe that was the reason that few people jumped between the job fields. On the other hand, people who had not jumped the job fields could not understand the difficulties one would face when he or she jumped the job field. Nevertheless, it seemed that all the high-level managers in the US had changed jobs several times in their life. In many ways, I felt that I had three different lives in the career side of my life.

I think the six years I spent in New Jersey was a valuable experience that eventually took me to a high-level management position in the federal government.

Chapter 13
UGA Bulldogs

When I got the call from the dean of agriculture from UGA, I was curious about the division chair position there. With some research, I found that the division consisted of three departments: the teaching and research department at Athens, the experiment station research department at Griffin, and the extension department at Athens. The Griffin department head reported to both the division chair and the AES station director at Griffin. The extension department head reported to the division chair and the associate dean of extension. The division chair represented all department operations at the annual budget negotiations with the dean, the director of residential instruction, the director of GA AES, and the director of extension. The division chair also handled all the promotion, tenure, and salary increases of all faculty members in the division. It was an interested and complicated matrix management system.

Dr. Tommy Nakayama was twelve years ahead of me at Berkeley, and he had the same PhD dissertation adviser as I did. I called him, as he was the department head of the research department at Griffin. I asked, "Hi, Tommy, I have been nominated for your division chair position. Why did you not apply for the position? You are much more qualified than me."

He said to me, "Joe, this is Deep South country. They never had a Yankee to be the division chair, much less a foreign national or nationalized American citizen." His answer actually raised my curiosity and provided a challenge for me to break another glass ceiling.

Besides searching for all the faculty member backgrounds in the food science and technology division, I called a mentor of mine at USDA, who happened to be the national program staff at CSREES in charge of reviewing food science programs at the land-grant universities. He said, "Joe, you are in luck. I just reviewed the UGA food science and technology (FST) program two weeks ago and am working on the report. I can send you a confidential copy of the report next week." He added, "One of UGA's problem from the federal point of view is that they need to diversify their leadership's background. I think you should apply for the job."

With the information on hand, I called the dean of UGA and accepted the invitation to be a candidate and sent in all needed materials and references. Shortly afterward, I was told that I made the short list and was one of the candidates that were invited to the campus for the interview process. Tommy Nakayama told me the composition of the twenty-plus members of the selection committee as well as the background of the dean, the director of the Georgia AES, the director of the extension, and the director of residential instruction. I was well prepared for the interview process.

The second book published by Joseph. It was the American Chemical Society Symposium Series number 405. (Taken in 1988 Los Angeles, California, US.)

Two major concepts that I used for the interview process were as follows: First, the three parts of the division—the teaching, the research, and the extension must be one entity and must cooperate with each other as a united division. Second, the division served the people of Georgia, of the US, and of the world—in that order. Also, I emphasized that the division chair must not only work with the faculty, staff, and students of the division, but he must also work with the alumni, the food industry, and other food science programs in the country and the world. My three-day interview process went well. Many were surprised that I knew the FST division so well and seemed to have good plans to administer the division.

Shortly after the interview process, the dean called me and offered me the job. I told him my salary at Campbell and expected that he would not be able to match it. I was surprised that he came back with an offer that matched my salary at Campbell. Although UGA did not offer moving costs, he gave me two weeks' additional salary as a compensation of moving from New Jersey to Georgia. After talking it over with my wife, we decided to accept the offer. To this date, I still did not know who nominated me to apply for the position.

I started the job soon after my acceptance of the position. I drove one of our cars to Athens and brought a condo, which was only five-minute drive from the food science building. I spent long hours at work for the first four months. Our house at Cherry Hill was finally sold, and we brought a new house in Athens in a new subdivision called River Bottom. Salina and Jeffrey moved to Athens before the Christmas of 1986. We started a new life in the Southern US again.

The teaching and research department at Athens had ten faculty members. Nine of them were white males. I later hired the first female faculty in the history of the department. I also brought in a marine extension staff to be the product development instructor and student club adviser. The student club won several Institute of Food Technologist (IFT) new products competition. The research department at Griffin had ten faculty members with two females. The extension department had four white males, for a total of twenty-four faculty in the division.

At UGA, the first thing I did was to interview each faculty member in the division and learned about their expertise, personal interests, capabilities, and goals. The second thing I did was to establish a weekly department meeting at Athens campus and a monthly division meeting that rotated between Athens and Griffin. The third thing I did was to hire two additional staff and relieved Athens faculty members of certain routine tasks for the department and the division. The fourth thing I did was to use the small amount of money left near the end of the 1986 budget cycle to purchase a word processor computer and a fax machine for the department. In the past, these funds would be divided to department faculty member to purchase things for their individual laboratory. The faculty members at Athens were not happy but did not want to upset me as the new department head. It was interesting that six month later, several faculty members came to my office and said, "I do not know how we can live without the fax machine. What a wonderful decision you made at the time."

It turned out that the faculty members were able to submit reports and proposals up to the last minute instead of having to mail these materials several days ahead of time and sometimes missed the deadlines. The staff members were happy to learn how to use the word processor and were able to turn out reports at a much faster speed than before. In other words, I won the trust of the faculty and the staff in a short time.

At the first college budget planning conference with the dean and the three associate deans, my major task was to negotiate with them about the allocation to the FST division from the federal and state budgets and the tenure and promotion of division faculty and staff members. At my first conference, I was able to convince them to add a staff position in my division for the handling of division budget.

I used my MBA expertise to train the newly hired accountant to set up a budget monitoring system so that I knew exactly how much funds were available in the division in real time. Faculty members were able to monitor their research project funds in real time as well. No one at the College of Agriculture at UGA had ever done that.

The deans were happy to see their investment paid off nicely, so they were good to me in budget allocations for the later years.

Joseph was elected as Fellow of the Institute of Food Technologists located at Chicago, Illinois on March 26, 1992.

I also used industry donations to hire a computer technician to assist the faculty, staff, and student to solve their computer problems. I also started an annual retreat for the division members before the college budget planning session. With a totally transparent financial system in the division, everyone was cooperative, was happy, and understood how to build and strengthen the division.

The Athens FST department had two pilot plants—a general processing pilot plant and a meat pilot plant. Both of these had wonderful staff that kept the facility in good shape and assisted to train students and make processed products for sale. I still recalled the delicious vermilion sausages from the meat pilot plant were always a hit during Christmas time.

During my six years at UGA, the State of GA experienced huge budget problems. I recalled that at least two times, all the state employees were asked to take voluntary leave without pay for several days. As such, all divisions in the college were trying to shrink the number of faculty members to meet budget shortages. My division was the exception. I wanted to expand the faculty, and I agreed with the animal science division head to transfer the dairy science program, with their three faculty members, to the FST division, together with the environmental health program, with two faculty members as well. I also worked with marine science program to transfer a staff to my department. Therefore, the FST department at Athens had sixteen faculty members within two years after my arrival at UGA.

One budget-saving management tool of the college was to eliminate and move the extension departments into the teaching and research departments in Athens. Three of the extension faculty members were transferred to the FST department and made it a total of nineteen faculty members. By the time I left UGA, the division had two departments and twenty-nine faculty members and had become one of the major FST programs in the US.

Two of the best hires I did at UGA was the hiring of Mike Doyle, from the University of Wisconsin, to replace Tommy Nakayama as department head at Griffin, and Casimir Akoh from Auburn U. Doyle formed a food safety center and transformed it into a world-renowned power in the field in a short period of time. Casimir Akoh was the best African American food science faculty in the nation and an expert in oil chemistry. I was the only division chair that carried research program and had my own research laboratory. It was well-equipped with new HPLC due to my human nutrition grant from the USDA. I offered Akoh the position as well as my laboratory to him. He just could not resist such an offer.

In addition to the size of the faculty members, by using the young assistant professors to replace the retired and left full professors, the Athens department had six full professors, six associate professors, and six assistance professors when I left it in 1992. The stabilized situation gave the division a great base to develop into one of the most highly respected and balanced teaching, research, and extension FST programs in the US and the world.

A scary thing took placed in 1988. My office had florescent lights hanging from the ceiling and were only held by some wires. One day, I was out of my office, and one of the double florescent lights fell from the ceiling and hit my chair where I normally would sit. I guess the Lord was looking after me, as he did all my life. I could have been killed or seriously hurt if I were sitting in the chair at the time.

Another thing I did at UGA was to interview each PhD students after they completed their degree requirements. I was able to learn the insight of their faculty advisers and learned their strengths and weakness. I would be able to assist some of the students to find good jobs and develop their career. One of the students I interviewed was a Greek student. He later became a department head and a college dean at major land-grant universities. Once, in a public meeting, he mentioned my interview with him.

He said that I walked out from my desk and told him, "You could be just like me." It gave him the inspiration to try academia administration instead of just be a professor.

I also found sponsors and established scholarships for graduate students, mainly to assist minority students with financial difficulties. Many students remembered me for that and told me so when we met again later in life. One interesting scholarship was donated by the Candy Manufacturers Association. They wanted to pay the donation in four years. The UGA Foundation said that it was against their policy and demanded that the association paid the whole donation up front. I told the foundation staff that I would open a personal account to accept the donation and did not need their service. The foundation caved in and accepted the donation in installments.

We enjoyed our house at River Bottom. It was a huge four-bedroom house with over four thousand square feet plus an unfinished attic, which could be made into two additional bedrooms. Salina spent much of the time cleaning the house, and I spent whatever the time I had in the yard. I recalled that we planted over five hundred azalea trees under the pine trees. One time during a strong storm, one of the pine trees in the neutral access area of our house and our next-door neighbor fell down. Luckily for us, it went to our neighbor's side. The tree cut through part of their bedroom and living room. It took the insurance company quite a while to rebuild their house. At this house, we got around with the neighbors well. We also entertained in the house often. One time, we hosted the whole division faculty members and had over thirty people in our house for desserts and drinks.

Pauline did not spend much time at our house at Athens. She was busy studying at Northwestern University (NU) in Evanston, Illinois. After two years as a pre-med major, she decided that the medical profession did not fit her personality and changed her major to clinical psychology.

Jeffrey went through his junior and senior high school years at Athens. He liked to attend UGA football games. The mascot of the team was a bulldog. His love of sports made him develop a strong interest in journalism and made him a sportswriter for several newspapers in his later life. The UGA football program was very rich due to the faithful followers from all over Georgia. The football program's income supported all the other men and women athletic teams at UGA. They also made donations to build the university library and athletic dormitory. Upon high school graduation, Jeffrey was accepted by Georgia Institute of Technology (GA Tech) and lived in Atlanta for one semester. He did not adjust to the big-city living well and came back to UGA for the second semester of his freshman year.

We were happy at Athens and enjoyed our life there and thought this could be where we would spend the rest of our lives, until one day, a letter from CA changed all that plan.

CHAPTER 14
Cal Poly's Learn by Doing

After nearly six years as division chair and department head at UGA, one day, I received a letter that urged me to apply for the position of dean of agriculture at California Polytechnic State University (Cal Poly), located at San Luis Obispo, CA. I had never heard of the school and was curious about it. Upon some research, I found that Cal Poly was the flagship campus of the California State University (CSU) system. The campus had a learn-by-doing philosophy, which emphasized hands-on learning. It also had the third-largest agriculture program in the US based on the number of students. It did not have PhD program and only offered bachelor of science and master's degree in all fields of agriculture. What impressed me was that it had a huge agribusiness (AGB) program. Cal Poly alumni were spread all over the country, particularly in California. It could be said that not a single agribusiness in CA did not have one of Cal Poly graduates. I decided to send in my application.

Shortly afterward, I was informed that I was selected to be interviewed on campus. In preparation of the interview process, I read the strategic plan of the college, searched for learn-by-doing examples, and checked out the faculty composition and famous alumni. I prepared a wonderful slide presentation outlining my management philosophy with several examples of how to emphasize learn by doing to the students, faculty, and administration. Also, the CA state government was facing severe budget cuts at the time. The university relied heavily on state-allocated funds for operation. Thus, I put in some thoughts for fundraising activities to assist the college operation and to reach out to alumni and the CA agricultural industry to assist the college.

My interview went well. During my presentation, someone asked the question, "How can we weather the budget cut?"

My answer was "When there is a will, there is a way!"

Another question was "What do you know about learn by doing?"

My answer was that I was born in China. The Chinese believe in life's experience. Thus, learning by doing was in my blood. Both answers apparently pleased many people in the audience. After the presentation, one old-time faculty member commented to his colleagues, "I have been here for twenty-five years. I thought I know what is learn by doing, but he seems to know it better than I."

I was offered the job with a reasonable salary. However, the living cost at San Luis Obispo was much higher than Athens. For example, one had to spend more than double the money to get less than two-third of the housing space at Athens. Thus, I demanded a higher salary. It turned out that the president really wanted me, so he petitioned to the CSU chancellor's office to provide me with a salary that was above the ceiling for the college deans set by the CSU system. He got approval, and I accepted the job. I drove from Athens to San Luis Obispo by myself in late August. I rented a studio in Morro Bay, which was ten miles away from my office at Cal Poly.

Thus, on September 1, 1992, I officially became the dean of agriculture at Cal Poly. The CA state government cut the higher education budget by 25 percent that year. Cal Poly was faced with eliminating either the College of Agriculture or the College of Professional Studies. When the president decided to hire me, he also decided to eliminate the College of Professional Studies. The largest program in the College of Professional Studies was the home economic programs. The food and nutrition program and ROTC unit were transferred to the College of Agriculture. The textile program was transferred to the College of Business, as part of the industrial business program. The interior design program was transferred to the College of Architecture, and the psychology program was transferred to the College of Liberal Arts.

Joseph's quarterly newsletter, Cal Poly Agri-view, Spring
1999 issue, at San Luis Obispo, CA, US

At the same time, the CSU system announced a golden handshake retirement program to encourage faculty and staff who were near retirement to take an early retirement. It happened that one of the two associate deans at the College of Agriculture took the handshake program. I asked the VP of academic affairs to assist me to replace the retired associate dean, but I had no budget to pay it. To my surprise, he agreed to have his director of institutional planning fill my associate dean position. He even agreed to carry the salary for one year. I could not believe my luck but later learned that the VP and the director did not agree on several institutional plans. Since the director carried a similar rank as the associate dean, it was hard for the VP to move the director. Therefore, I gave VP an opportunity to get rid of a headache while at the same time, he did me a favor that he could ask for payback in the future.

During the first week when I was the dean, I established a weekly meeting with the department heads. I also interviewed each department head to learn about their programs and problem areas. I found that the college was very fragmented. Each department operated on their own. There was no unity as a college. The previous dean did not want to make hard decisions. He left the decision to the faculty and department head committees. The acting dean, during the search of the dean, did the same. The faculty members and department heads all preferred to continue in that mode of operation, but not me.

At the first all-college meeting before the start of the fall quarter, I told everybody that we would establish a major goal of the college: "We want to be the best teaching College of Agriculture in the nation." I also said that we must unite as one entity and not as ten separate departments. I told them of an old Chinese story about a dying wealthy old man. He called his five sons to his bedside and handed each of them a pair of chopsticks. He asked them to break it, and they all could easily do it. Then he put five pairs of chopsticks together and asked them to break it. None of them could do it. He then said to his sons, "When you are on your own, you are very fragile and can easily be broken and lose all your wealth. When you are united together, you become a strong unit, and no one can shake your wealth." To be a strong college, we must unite as one unit, and each department would eventually be stronger than before.

When I was appointed, one of the fears of the college faculty members was that I would turn the college into a research program like the many land-grant institutes that were in my background. The faculty were very proud of the fact that Cal Poly was a learn-by-doing teaching institute and that most of the faculty members were excellent teachers and not spending anytime in research activities.

I asked some faculty members what evidences they had to prove that they were great teachers. Did any of the faculty members ever win national teaching awards? The answers to both questions were "None." I told them that it was not good enough to say that we were great teachers ourselves. We needed to take steps to have other people in the field and around the nation to recognize that we had good, excellent, and great teachers. To start with, we needed to establish some teaching awards in the college. Winning college teaching award would be the first step toward winning national teaching awards.

During my meetings with agricultural industry and alumni in the state, I asked them to consider making small commitments of sponsoring outstanding teaching faculty members. While I was at it, I also asked some corporations to consider sponsoring staff awards. Within weeks, I received enough commitments to establish ten teaching awards for $1,000 each and six staff awards for $500 each.

To top things off, I thought of a unique learn-by-doing award. The CEO of Dole packaged food was a member of my college advisory council. During my visit to his company, I proposed to him to establish such an award. My idea was that the award winner would be given a chance to visit one of the Dole's international locations to learn about the operation at the location. Upon return to campus, the faculty member would give a seminar to the college faculty members and students on what he or she learned from the experience. The CEO was so intrigued about the idea that he immediately agreed to sponsor such an award. To make the award more attractive, he included the winner's partner or a family member in the paid travel plus some spending money. He also agree to sponsor a staff award for the staff to visit one of Dole's domestic location and make report upon return to campus.

The first time the faculty and staff award were passed out, we had a celebration event. The Dole's CEO personally selected the award trophy. It was a crystal flame on a wooden stand, with relevant carving about the winner. He also gave the college a huge crystal flame trophy to record the yearly winners. We placed it in the college conference room. I also had the yearly winners of the faculty and staff award plaques hung on the college conference room walls. All of a sudden, the spirit of teaching filled the college and spread to the whole Cal Poly campus.

To sharpen the teaching skills of some of the teachers, I asked the local Dale Carnegie Institute instructor to design a training course for our faculty and staff members. I raised the needed funds for the course. Alumnus Al Smith donated half of the cost. Thirty faculty and staff members volunteered to receive the training that focused on teaching skills and student relationship. The course enhanced the cooperation spirit among the participating faculty and staff from different departments. The course also enhanced the unity among them, which led to several cross-department projects.

On a visit to a branch campus of the University of Minnesota (UMN), I learned that the whole campus was linked with computers. The particularly impressive part of the system to me was their teaching computer laboratory. I talked with our faculty and staff about it, and we did not have any fund to try it. One AGB faculty was very handy in fixing computers. He volunteered his time and worked with his students on weekends to build a teaching computer laboratory. We took two adjacent classrooms to build the laboratory. The design of the laboratory was unique in that the students had a U-shaped seating. The student seats could be rotated. When the instructor gave the lecture, the students would face the instructor and had the computer at their back. When the instructor told the students to work on the computer, the students would rotate their seats and face the computer. The beauty of this setup was that the instructor could see all the screens of the students and monitored their work progress. No students could play games on the computers. I also got two gifts for the laboratory. First was a set of the most advanced computers from the Hewlett-Packard CEO, who was the chair of the advisory council of the College of Engineering. He heard about my project and donated the computers. Second was from a software company owned by a College of Business alumnus who was developing a unique software so that the instructors could separate the students into groups to work on different problems. Thus, no student could copy from their neighbors on examinations or projects. The instructor could also ask any student to take over the class computers to show how he or she was solving a problem. The Cal Poly's VP of facility provided all the electrical and wiring supports to us without charge. The teaching laboratory was built in a very short period of time, without any cost to the college. Some faculty members adapted the teaching styles very quickly. We also added distance learning capacity of the laboratory so it could be used for sharing the teaching with other universities and our Swanton Pacific Ranch. Later on, other Cal Poly colleges and others in the CSU campuses copied our project, but we were the inventor of this unique teaching style.

Joseph received citation from student showing college logo
on May 7, 2001 at San Luisao Obispo, CA, US

My first experience of meeting the Cal Poly alumni was a testy one. A prominent alumnus invited me to visit his office in Salinas, California. He also invited several other area alumni, including Al Smith, the owner of Swanton Pacific Ranch. During dinnertime, they asked me all kinds of questions; many of them were similar to the questions I had from the interview process. The major one was "What do you know of learn by doing and about your plan to revive it in the College of Agriculture at Cal Poly?"

I had no problem answering all the questions. I also told them about my idea of teaching excellence and the Learn by Doing award. Cal Poly's VP of instruction went with me and commented on our way back that he thought we were at a TV talk show and I was the one with all the answers.

The CA state budget cuts made me realized that we needed to develop other resources to support the college operations and student services. The alumni meeting gave me the idea of untapped resources. I first hired a recently retired AGB faculty member on a part-time basis as the college advancement officer. He gathered information about where we had large concentrations of alumni in CA. I started to visit these locations and met with small groups of alumni and industry friends to share my idea of contributing resources to the college. Very quickly, I found out that the alumni were very disappointed with the current Cal Poly administration for deemphasizing learn by doing. The part-time alumni decided that he could not do more as he was not a professional fundraiser. I decided to hire Mike Barr, who was the advancement director of the Business College of CSU-Fresno. He was able to find a big donor and had their college named after the donor. Since he was the first advancement director at the college level, the university was unhappy about it and placed a low salary limit so that I could not hire him. I decided to raise donation and hired Mike Barr with the Cal Poly foundation fund, which was outside the university salary system. Mike and I developed a unique logo for the college and made various small materials, such as coffee cups, luggage tags, and magnets with the college logo and "Learn by Doing" printed on them. The university office prohibited me to use the Cal Poly in a stylish form, saying they had a patent on it. So I designed to put the university mascot in between the words and put "Agriculture" below a line. It was so beautiful that many people loved it, and we got many requests for the small gifts.

I told Mike Barr to organize the biggest rodeo gathering with Cal Poly alumni, which we had hoped the president could attend, but he did not. However, the president did attend the green-and-gold wine tasting event at Napa Valley, which was sponsored by our alumni. Many donors liked my position that "The College of Agriculture was the origin of and would always be the home of learn by doing." Alumni donations came in quickly, and many made sure their donations were for learn-by-doing activities in the College of Agriculture only.

To further connect with the alumni, I asked Mike Barr to rent a bus and carry college faculty and staff to visit industries at various CA locations. One bus visited Southern CA, including Bakersfield, where we visited Rain for Rent, Nestlé's ice cream lines, and the largest carrot processing plant; and then we went to Santa Maria, where the vegetable processing and cold storage facility was, and to the San Luis Obispo farm bureau and the largest farm shop in the Central Coast. The other bus visited one of the largest dairy facilities in the Central Coast area near Fresno, Modesto's Gallo Winery, Merced's Foster Farm chicken processing plant, and Swanton Pacific Ranch. The faculty members learned about other agricultural industries outside their teaching area and became better teachers, while the alumni were energized connecting with the old and new faculty members of their student days. Bob Gallo was so intrigued with our spirit that he provided us with bottles of the Turning Leaf wine one month before it was for sale on the market. The Gallo connection eventually led to a 150-acre Gallo vineyard on the college farm ground.

Communication was very important in the management of a large unit like the Cal Poly's College of Agriculture. I practiced open communication to all faculty, staff, and students in the college. Each month, I wrote an open letter to them, with all important matters taking place in the university, the college, and with the alumni gathering. It was so popular that many faculty and staff of other colleges asked our folks for a copy of the newsletter. I also held weekly department head meetings right after the VP of instruction held the dean's meeting. From time to time, I would attend the department faculty meeting without announcement ahead of time. I held monthly staff meeting without any faculty presence. Once a month, I held a student breakfast meeting with one faculty and one staff member so the students could ask questions about the college, the department, or on university affairs. There was never a college dean who practiced this type of open communication as I did at Cal Poly. The results were that the college operated as one unit, and everyone understood that I put the college's benefit ahead of anything else. Everyone in the college started to trust me and made my management of the college with ease.

One last thing that I brought to college was a multicultural program. Due to the high entrance standard of Cal Poly, the minority enrollment of Hispanic and Asian students to the university and the college was very low in comparison with other CSU campuses. I talked to our folks and asked one Japanese American agriculture engineering faculty to set up a multicultural program room. Faculty members of various departments could volunteer to stay at the room to provide free consulting and assistance to minority students. Some faculty could even assist the students to solve their social problems in the university. I invited the director of UC Berkeley Hispanic program to our college to meet with our students. He brought with him his advisory group of Hispanic business owners twice.

After the meeting, one advisory member told me, "Dr. Jen, agriculture is in our blood. You are our hero."

The numbers of Hispanic student applicants to the college increased quickly, and within one year, the minority enrollment in the college was four times higher than the rest of the university. Later, I was told that the Hispanic students gave me a nickname, Papa Jen.

With efforts, I had lots of fun managing the college at Cal Poly. Every year, I had some new program taking place so the college was always making improvement in one way or another. As I reflected on my career at Cal Poly, I think my influence lasted for thirty years: I was dean for nine years; Dave Weiner, whom I hired as associate dean, was dean for ten years; and Andy Thulin, whom I hired as animal science department head, was acting dean one year and the dean for ten years. He is still the dean of the college to date. It was quite satisfying that I had such a long-lasting influence in a very unique program.

CHAPTER 15

Outside Accomplishment at Cal Poly

Besides handling matters inside the College of Agriculture, I had lots of outside activities. First and foremost was the establishment of alumni connections. It brought me to all parts of CA to connect with many alumni. I also established friendship with many CEOs and directors of CA agricultural companies.

As the new dean of agriculture at Cal Poly, I attended the annual meeting of deans and directors of agriculture of the US. I was surprised to find out that among nearly two hundred deans and directors, only four minorities, besides the ones from Black colleges, were present. The four included three women and me. There were no ethnic minorities besides me. As the federal laws required diversity, I was quickly being appointed to fifteen national and Western regional committees. It kept me really busy, attending many of the meetings. However, it also gave me the opportunity to spread the reputation of Cal Poly and our learn-by-doing philosophy among the other universities and colleges, big or small.

My other significant activity was to serve on the advisory board of the CA Department of Food and Agriculture (CDFA.) The advisory board consisted of fifteen members who were mostly CA agricultural industry leaders. Two members were from the academia, one each from the UC and the CSU systems. Two at-large members represented the environment and consume groups. All members were appointed by the CA governor for a four-year term. The board met once a month at Sacramento, the site of the CA state government. The three-hour meetings discussed the important matters affecting the CA agricultural industries, oftentimes related to the CDFA regulations, rules, and guidelines. The top officers of CDFA divisions were present most of the time as participants. The secretary of CDFA served as cochairperson with an industry leader. The secretary was Ms. Ann Veneman at the time. Ms. Veneman was a graduate of UC Davis and had a law degree from UC Berkeley. When she was first appointed as the secretary, she naturally thought that UC Davis should be the institute respected by the CA agricultural industries. She was surprised to find out that it was not the case. Instead, everyone pointed out the graduates of Cal Poly were the main source of agricultural industry workers and managers. When she met me and after understanding the learn-by-doing philosophy, she became a believer of the philosophy. Little did I know that she would be the one who would recommend me to work for the US federal government.

Joseph was lead lecturer at Sino-American Symposium on Agricultural
R&D in China in October, 1996 at Beijing, China

Besides the above activities, I had many other outside programs and activities. The three projects that I enjoyed the most were the Swanton Pacific Ranch, the agriculture ambassador, and the Gallo wine-grape projects.

Al Smith's father started the Orchard Hardware Store from his garage and grew it into a seven hundred chain stores in CA and certain Western US states. Al did not like the hardware business that he inherited from his father. Since he was an environmentalist, he sold the hardware business and used the fund to purchase three thousand acres of land north of Santa Cruz on Highway 1. He also used the leftover fund to buy five hundred acres of virgin forest land in the inland of Santa Cruz. He built a few houses at the ranch and used the land for raising cows and crops. He also built a one-mile-long railroad for his collection of one-third-scale railway trains. He attended Cal Poly but did not graduate with a degree. He went on to take some business courses at Stanford University. Since he was not married and had no children, he wanted to give the land to either Cal Poly or Stanford upon his death. His only condition was that the land could not be sold for cash and must be maintained as it was in the native state. He petitioned the Santa Cruz County and got approved to name his land Swanton Pacific. He built a home on the top of his land, which could view the ocean over the hills. He asked Cal Poly to assist in the landscaping of his house. The associate dean of agriculture at the time was a strong-minded person and did not get along with Al. When I first visited Al at his farm, he told me that the associate dean moved his favorite roses without consultation with him. Thus, he changed his mind in giving the ranch to Cal Poly and approached Stanford University. Stanford did not want to be bothered with the management of the ranch and would only accept it if they could sell it for cash. During my first visit with him, I told him I would change the college contact person with him and said to him, "Wow, you have the only cows that have their own ocean view." He liked it very much, and we got along great. I asked an animal science faculty member to work with him using his life experience to substitute for some of the needed course and assisted him to write a senior project, so he received a BS degree from Cal Poly. He proudly displayed the degree certificate in the center of his living room. I also remembered that when I was in Hawaii, I met the ranch manager of the largest ranch in the Big Island. He was a Cal Poly alumnus and was looking for a project that he could do to assist Cal Poly. I designed a project that he would ship his piglets to Swanton Pacific Ranch for a six-month stay. When they reached marketing age, they were to ship the cows back to Hawaii. I was not sure if it made economic sense to do so, but it satisfied his desire to help Cal Poly and give the students the chance to practice learn by doing. I also established a separate Cal Poly foundation account to handle profits made at Swanton Pacific from its cow and crop business. The fund could only be used to build up Swanton Pacific Ranch and for students' benefits.

It also turned out that when Dr. Wally Mark, who was a natural resource management (NMR) faculty, was done with his one-year loan from the VP of instruction, I made him the director of Swanton Pacific Ranch with the foundation fund. Wally established a student base at Swanton as all NMR majors had to spend one quarter at Swanton forest area to learn how to manage the forestry land. We also build a distance learning facility there so the students could take regular NMR courses at Swanton Ranch via distance learning. When Al found that he was sick with only six months to live, he decided to sign the contract with me to give the ranch to the college.

Several months later, Al passed away peacefully in his mountaintop home. I hosted a memorial service on campus and made some memorial items for guests. The uniquely designed coffee cup was so well-liked by everybody that Cal Poly president used it as his daily coffee cup till his retirement. I also used some of the foundation fund to rebuild the two-room faculty club next to the president's house and named it as Al Smith Conference Building. Any faculty or student could rent the building for small group activities. The building was managed by Cal Poly foundation and could only cater foods from the foundation, who handled all the eating outfits on campus.

The building had been very popular, due to the location in the center of the campus, that often, it had a waiting list. This was the story of Al Smith.

Cal Poly College of Agriculture had an agriculture ambassador program managed by the agricultural education (AE) department. The selected AE students used to visit the CA junior colleges and high schools. The idea was to recruit students to major in AE, and upon graduation, the graduates could return to be agriculture teachers at these schools. When I became dean, I felt the program should be used to recruit students for all majors. I asked the faculty in charge of the program to allow students of other majors to apply to be ambassadors. AGB students responded quickly, and soon, half of the ambassadors were AGB students. I then made two additional changes. First, I provided each ambassador with a tailor-made high-quality jacket with the college logo on it. Second, I started to use them as campus guides to VIP visitors.

I learned that the local Dale Carnegie Institute instructor was a Cal Poly alumnus who wanted to assist the college. I told him about the agriculture ambassador program. He was very interested in the idea and agreed to provide a special training class for the ambassadors free of charge. The students would meet once a week for three hours, for a twelve-week class. They learned about public speaking, presentation skills, and service as a campus guide to potential students and VIP visitors. The ambassadors were taught to present the learn-by-doing experiences at Cal Poly. Their special outfits at events made them the center of attention. Quickly, the academic quality of the ambassadors increased. Many campus VIP visitors liked them and often provided potential intern and job opportunities to them. The program was totally supported from outside donations. The reputation of our agriculture ambassadors made many CA universities and colleges form the same types of teams. We started an annual meeting of the agriculture ambassadors on campus each spring to share successful activities with each other. The students had a good time, and the college had more applicants and donors.

When I hired Mark Barr as the college advancement director, the University Advancement Office told us that we were not allowed to contact the E. J. Gallo Winery because Tom Gallo, who played linebacker in Cal Poly football games, had been making donations to the athletic program. The college had an alumnus who served as the president of the American Farmland Foundation. When he scheduled their tenth-year celebration for the board members of his foundation at Pacifica, at the Golden Gate Park in San Francisco, he asked me to make a ten-minute presentation about the learn-by-doing philosophy. I did and many of the board members were impressed and asked many questions.

Afterward, Bob and Marie Gallo came up to me. Marie said to me that her son Tom had been working with Cal Poly athletic program, and I said, "Yes, I am aware of that."

Bob said, "Actually, we are more interested in your agriculture program than the athletic program." He asked me if Cal Poly had any viticulture and wine program.

I said no, we only had a faculty member who taught a viticulture course. However, we had a strong wine marketing program. A couple of months later, I was invited to attend the CA wine gala event in Sacramento. Bob Gallo saw me and said that he had a project that was trying to use the pomace of the grapes and did not have any luck finding a solution. He asked me whether Cal Poly could work on it. I said we had an enterprise project for students to work on real-world projects. He asked how much it would cost him. I said $5,000. He could not believe it and said that he had given UC Davis and Cornell University a sizable grant money, and their faculty members were not able to come up with a solution for the past two years. He asked how long our enterprise project would last. I said three to six months. He immediately wrote me a check to fund the project. I asked a wine marketing faculty member to gather six AGB, horticulture, and food science students to form a team. I personally served as the adviser to the team. I recalled that when I was at Campbell, I had a project working on reducing the solid mass of carrot juice pomace with commercial enzymes. The project was not successful because while we did reduce the solid mass, the enzyme digestion left a bitter taste, so the additional pressed juice could not be used in V8 juice formulation. However, we were able to use the reduced pomace as animal feed and reduced the landfill charges for the company. The students performed the Gallo grape pomace experiments and obtained good results. Since Gallo was interested in reducing the pomace only, we did not have to worry about the bitter taste problem. When the students presented the result to Bob Gallo, he was very surprised and immediately hired two of the students as interns for his company. He asked me if I would be interested in building a grape vineyard at Cal Poly. He had been interested in finding a testing place to grow some of the grape varieties in the CA Central Coast area. I agreed to send him a proposal in a week. I outlined a project that Gallo would provide all the grapes, the equipment needed to construct the vineyard, the weather stations, etc. The estimated cost to him would be in the millions of dollars. In addition, I asked his staff to teach courses to our students and purchase the harvested grape at a preset price to make wines. Cal Poly would provide 150 acres of land with his choice on our farms, water used for irrigation, and our farm staff to maintain the vineyard. After twenty-five years, the vineyard would become the property of Cal Poly. He agreed to the proposal. However, when I presented the project to the university for approval, we ran into a problem. Technically, the university land belonged to the State of CA and was not allowed to be used and managed by outside entity. We also could not sell the land, as any funds raised by the land sale would go to the general fund of the state government and could not be turned back to Cal Poly. I was very disappointed.

A couple of weeks later, since I served as the secretary of the Cal Poly foundation, I asked the director of the foundation whether the foundation could work with

Gallo on the project. He said the foundation probably could do it, but there was never such a kind of case in the past. He searched the foundation bylaws and said to me that there was no guideline against it. I turned to the university and asked, "What if we loaned the land to the foundation, and the foundation worked with Gallo to build the vineyard?" It was a project beneficial to the students, and it fitted in with our learn-by-doing philosophy. The university was not able to find any guideline against the idea but said that they needed to forward the idea to the CSU chancellor's office for approval. The chancellor was excited about the idea and presented it to the CSU board of trustees for comments. Members of the trustees were mostly business executives, and they loved the idea. When the trustee scheduled this project for discussion at their meeting, it became public knowledge.

The president of UC system learned about it and asked Bob Gallo, who was a member of the president's board of advisers and a personal friend. He asked Bob Gallo, "Why do you want to build the vineyard at Cal Poly? I have the world-famous viticulture and wine department at UC Davis and several experiment stations throughout CA. If you build the vineyard on our campus ground, I will double your investment so we can have the best vineyard of the country."

Bob Gallo realized that whatever reason he gave, the president would have answers to rebut him. He just smiled and said, "I understand everything, except that Cal Poly has this guy named Joe Jen, and I just like him." End of the conversation.

The project took six months for the lawyers of Gallo company, Cal Poly administration, and Cal Poly foundation to iron out all the details for the agreement. Meanwhile, Bob Gallo took helicopter rides onto our Cal Poly farm grounds twice, did a number of soil analysis, tested the weather conditions, and eventually located the 150 acres of land of his choice. He was determined to make the project work, and it did. During the preparation period, the CNN news reported the project twice as examples of how academic universities and industries could work together to teach real-world skills to the students. This was the Gallo story.

As you could see, my outside accomplishments were closely tied to my job as the dean of the college. At the same time, they satisfied my interests and challenges. It just added more fun to the job.

CHAPTER 16
Chances to Leave Cal Poly

Not even one year since my arrival at Cal Poly, I received an invitation to apply for the VP and provost positions at the Cal State Eureka campus. I was surprised at the invitation and found out I was nominated by the agriculture dean at Cal State Pomona. Since I had just arrived at Cal Poly and was not interested in university administrative duties, I declined the invitation. Later on, when I asked the Pomona dean about the nomination, he just said that he felt that I was more than just an agriculture dean material.

In the subsequent years, I received two more invitations to apply for the VP and provost positions at other CSU campuses and declined them both. I also received an invitation to apply for the VP and agriculture dean positions at the new UC campus at Merced when it was established as the tenth campus of the UC system. I did not apply.

However, I did apply to an invitation to be the agriculture dean at the University of Hawaii (UH), partly due to curiosity and partly to honor my nominee, the department head of the food science and technology at the UH. It turned out to be an interesting experience.

After I submitted the application material and did the video interview, I was selected to be one of the three final candidates invited for campus interview. I was excited to visit the Hawaiian Islands. What I did not realized was that Hawaii was the most democratic state of the union. The interview was a week-long event. In addition to visiting the main campus at Honolulu, I was taken to three other islands and met the faculty, staff, students, and alumni at those locations. In all, I met nearly one thousand people, and I was told that each of them had a vote on the three final candidates.

As my usual practice, I made careful preparation for the interview and had two major points for future development of the agriculture program at UH. The two major points that I made at my presentation to the audience were that UH needed to build a niche program that made it stand out among all agriculture programs in the nation. UH should not compete with other land-grant programs for subject matters, such as biotechnology, environmental care, and production agriculture. Instead, I proposed for UH to be a bridge of the East and West world and hold biweekly international symposiums and conferences of all subjects in agriculture programs. Since the UH already had an East and West Center for years, the logistics could easily be done. Hawaii, being in the middle of the East and West nations and a wonderful vacation place, many scientists, government officers, and industry personnel would all be interested in attending these symposiums and conferences. It would be more economical for participants from the US to go all the way to Asian countries to attend meetings and for Asian scientists to go to the forty-eight US continental states. The second point I made was that I would encourage UH to develop agricultural tourism using all the Hawaiian Islands. UH had one of the two colleges with tourism programs. It would be natural for the agricultural program to cooperate with the College of Tourism to develop a world-class agricultural tourism program.

Another surprise I had during the interview was that I met a number of Cal Poly alumina during my interview process. It seemed that UH had an old cooperation project with Cal Poly in the seventies and eighties. Many Hawaiians had attended Cal Poly fifteen to thirty years ago. These folks were all supporters of my candidacy to be the agriculture dean.

One week after my visit to the Hawaiian Islands, the VP and provost of UH called me and asked me to visit again, this time, with my wife, to look at the housing and location. So Salina and I made the trip. We found that the housing price at Honolulu was so high that the salary of the agriculture dean could not support us living in a single house. We would need to rent an apartment in Downtown Honolulu or live at the other side of the island and drive to work every day. I had an NTU classmate, Dr. C. S. Tang, who had been a professor of plant pathology at UH for over thirty years. He supplied me with many information when I prepared for the interview. He showed us his town where his house was. It was on the other side of Oahu via the cross-island highway over the mountain peak. Living on the other side of the island would not work for my job as a dean. One thing Salina was really concerned was the island fever. It was a five-hour plane ride to CA and another five-hour plane ride to the East Coast if we wanted to leave the island.

After much discussion, we decided not to accept the offer from the UH. Later on, I found out that I received nearly 80 percent of the votes among the three finalists, which never took place before. Years later, when we visited the Hawaiian Islands as tourists, there were still university staff or industry folks who remembered that I declined their offer for the deanship.

In the year 2000, I received a call from the provost of Iowa State University (ISU), indicating that I was nominated to apply for the agriculture dean of ISU. I could not resist the temptation to find out about the situation at a famous land-grant institute.

After a preliminary video interview, I was told that I made the short list of three candidates for campus interviews. I did my due diligence to prepare for the interview and made an impressive presentation of outlining how I would emphasize the teaching of undergraduates while at the same time encourage faculty members to develop new and innovative approaches to research and extension. The interview committee consisted of a large group of faculty, staff, alumni, and Iowa business leaders. One of the major concerns I did find out was that the associate dean of extension was also the VP of external affairs of the university. The dean only had control of the resident instruction and the research program of the college. The provost called me and asked me in what condition I would take the job. I told him of my concerns on extension and said I needed to have the extension be taken out of the VP's hand and put it into the dean's hand. The provost was new to ISU, and I was not sure that he presented my request to the president. So I ended up not being selected as the dean. Since I had the votes of all the young and progressive faculty, the staff, the alumni, the students, and the Iowa business leaders, the VP made the decision that none of the candidates could be selected as the dean.

On the way back from Iowa, I ran into Ms. Ann Veneman, who was at ISU for an economic conference. She said to me that she was not surprised that ISU could not tolerate a progressive dean like me. She also said that the VP of external affairs was a very difficult person to deal with. When I made it to DC, a colleague Under-Secretary of farm service was from Iowa. He knew everything about my visit and said to me, "Iowa's loss is the nation's gain."

Many years later, when I returned to Cal Poly after my DC experience, I received a call from the president of the CSU at the Eureka campus. It turned out that the president was the VP at ISU when I interviewed there. He told me about the situation at the time. The only group of faculty members that were opposing my appointment was a group of old faculty members who lived on federal grants. They were worried that I might force them to teach undergraduate students. Iowa did have strong congressional senators and congressmen, and these faculty members could live on the federal grants and had an easy life. The president at Eureka was interested in me being his provost, but I was not interested.

As you could see, I had some interesting opportunities to leave Cal Poly. Nevertheless, I did not want to leave. We enjoyed the California Central Coast living, and I was having a lot of fun at Cal Poly. We had planned to end my career and retire there. However, a call from DC changed all that.

SECTION 3

LIFE AT WASHINGTON, DC

CHAPTER 17

A Call from DC

My fifth career move was being selected as the Under-Secretary of research, education, and economics (REE) of the USDA. There are two kinds of federal employees: the regular career employees and the president-appointed political employees. The president-appointed political employees are the top managers. Sometimes, it is quite a challenge to manage the career employees. Since the regular employees may stay for a lifetime, therefore, if they do not like you, they can easily say yes to you on everything but not do anything. They can wait for you to be replaced in due time, as most political appointees do not stay in their positions more than two years. I lasted five years on the job, which was long by any standard. I liked the challenge and found that my position was very powerful. If I concentrated on the job and forgot about any political future, I could get a lot of meaningful projects done for the good of the citizens of the US and the world.

In January 2001, the new president George W. Bush announced several cabinet members. One of them was Ms. Ann Veneman for the Secretary of Agriculture. Ms. Veneman used to be the Secretary of the CDFA of California. She was the first female Secretary of Agriculture in the history of the USDA. When we learned about the news, I said to Salina, "We may get a phone call from DC with an invitation to work at USDA. However, of all the positions at USDA, I am only interested in one specific one. The position is so high that I do not think they will consider me for it." Two months passed, and there was no phone call. I thought that this time, my intuition was wrong.

Near the end of March, I had a meeting at the National Academy of Sciences (NAS) in DC for a project to evaluate the effectiveness of Cooperative Station of Research, Education and Economics Service (CSREES), a unit of USDA/REE. I was a member of the evaluation team, which was chaired by a senior faculty member of ISU. The day before I was to travel to DC, a phone call came in, and the caller identified himself as the Director of the White House Liaison Office of USDA. He asked if I could have lunch with him the next day. I asked what the meeting was for. He said that it was best that we discussed that face-to-face.

Two days later, I saw a young man at the restaurant. He came right out and said to me, "Secretary Veneman would like to nominate you as the Under-Secretary of REE. What do you think?"

I thought to myself, *My God, my intuition was correct after all.*

He went on to say that the salary of the position was 10 percent less than my current salary as the Dean of Agriculture at Cal Poly. The position was a presidential nomination, and US Congress confirmed position. It carried with it many restrictions. He went on to talk about the restrictions, but my mind was someplace else, and I did not hear everything he said. Finally, he said that although Secretary Veneman would nominate me as the candidate, whether the President would pick me to be nominated and sent to the US Congress and whether the US Senate would confirm me was not certain.

I knew that a position like this normally would attract a lot of candidates. Many senators, congressmen, industry groups, academic and research institutes, and Non-Government Organization (NGO) would all submit potential candidates to the White House. Most Secretaries of Agriculture would suggest several candidates for the President to pick the suitable one for political considerations. So I asked him how many candidates Secretary Veneman plan to submit to the White House? He replied that the Under-Secretary of REE required strong background in many areas. Secretary Veneman felt strongly of my abilities that she would send me as the only candidate to the White House for consideration. I asked how much time I had to think about the offer.

Joseph received an appreciate award from the Society of Chinese American Professors and Scientists in April of 2005 at Chicago, Illinois, US.

He said, "By noon tomorrow! If you decide to accept the invitation, you can go to the White House Personnel Office tomorrow afternoon to start a long process of being nominated."

I called Salina that night and discussed the invitation. On the one hand, I felt flattered that Secretary Veneman thought strongly of me, as if fate was calling on me. I knew that no Asian Americans had ever occupied the Under-Secretary level position at USDA. In fact, not even at the Deputy Under-Secretary level position. I felt a sense of mission to break the glass ceiling. On the other hand, I also knew that the position was a difficult one, with lots of challenges. Strangely enough, that thought made me excited, as I enjoy challenges. Salina was very supportive of me accepting the invitation and felt the same on the mission and the challenges.

The next day, I called the Director to accept the invitation. He told me the address of the White House Personnel Office and later called me that he had confirmed an appointment for me for the next day. When I reached the Office the next day, a young lady asked me some routine questions and handed me a big stack of papers. She told me to complete the forms as soon as possible.

It was interesting that during the meeting at NAS, the possible candidates of the Under-Secretary of REE were discussed at break time. Many members of the committee had their preferred candidates. Nevertheless, the consensus was that the Dean of Agriculture at Purdue University, who was the chair of the advisory council for the current Under-Secretary of REE, would be the top candidate.

I spent many hours filling out the forms given to me by the young lady. It was so detailed that I felt I had to write down everything about me since my birth. I needed to list all my close relatives, my academic trainings, and every job I ever had. I needed to fill in the names of my bosses and best friends and colleagues, my students, and my neighbors. When did my parents die? Every foreign trip I took in the past ten years, where did I go, how many days was I away, and why did I take the trips? There were detailed questions about my financial conditions—every stock I ever bought and sold, and anything I owned. It also asked about my personal hobby and when I started the hobby. I had filled out many forms in my life, but none could compare to these forms. I filled out the form the best I could and sent it by express mail to the White House personnel office.

Two weeks later, when I had to go to DC again for the NAS meeting, the lady at the White House Personnel Office called me and told me she had set up an appointment for me with her boss. When the time came, I went to the office again and found a middle-aged gentleman who greeted me with a handshake. Later, I learned that he was the Deputy Director of the White House Personnel Office. The first sentence he said to me was, "How come you are not a Republican?"

I was surprised but answered quickly, "I am the Dean of Agriculture at Cal Poly. One of the major jobs as the Dean is to gather donations from alumni. Half of my alumni were Republicans, and the other half were Democrats. If I was a

Republican, the Democratic alumni would hesitate to support my college fully. If I was a Democrat, the Republican alumni would hesitate to support my college whole-heartedly. Therefore, I am an independent, but I vote mostly like a Republican."

He laughed and said that it was the first time he ever heard the reasoning, but he said it made sense to him. It was a very practical way to get my job done. We talked for nearly an hour, mostly to confirm the answers I filled on the forms and a few pointed questions, such as if I had ever hired an illegal immigrant and if I liked to give parties. At the end, he told me that I passed the first round of the checkups for the candidacy. The FBI checkups would be next.

The following week, an FBI agent came to my house and talked to me for more than two hours. Sensing that I lived a clean life with nothing to hide, he complained to me at the end that normally, FBI would be given six months to complete a detailed security checkup like mine. This time, the White House asked them to do it in six weeks. A different agent came the next day to talk to Salina for two hours. The Cal Poly President was interviewed for two hours. Many of my former colleagues and students at the various universities were interviewed. Even my alma mater in Taiwan was checked. My neighbor told us that they were asked if we held wild parties, if we hired illegal immigrants as gardeners, and whether I was a womanizer. At the end, I probably passed the FBI check in flying colors. In late May, the White House informed me that the President had sent my nomination as the Under-Secretary of USDA/REE to the US Congress for consideration. The news reached local newspapers and several of the Chinese newspapers in the US. I got a number of calls from the media to interview me. One local news noted that, if confirmed, I would be the first cabinet-level appointee for the federal government, not only for Cal Poly but also for the entire CSU system.

It happened that Cal Poly asked the Secretary of Agriculture to be the commencement speaker for the 2001 spring commencement. She came in early June to give the commencement presentation. She mentioned my name. "We will just borrow your Agriculture Dean for a few years to go to Washington, DC, to assist me."

In mid-June, I was asked to be in USDA for a week of training to face the US Congressional confirmation process. They gave me a book by the Brookline Institute entitled *How to Pass the Congressional Interview of Presidential Appointment*. I was trained together with the proposed Deputy Secretary from Indiana. We had several mock sessions of congressional staff and noted lobbyist who were familiar with the confirmation hearing process. We were also asked to meet with the US congressional staff to check on our financial and other backgrounds. However, we did not get scheduled for the hearing in June, as expected. We were sent back to our home states for a few weeks. Finally, the call came that our congressional hearing was set for July 9, 2001.

I was allowed to invite my wife, my brother, my elder sister, and a good friend, Dr. Grace Lo, who replaced my younger sister to the hearing. It was a packed house with many reporters, lobbyists, and persons with special interests. Two Indiana congressmen made statements to support the Deputy Secretary. No one from CA showed up on my behalf. The Chair of the Senate Agricultural Committee was a Democrat from Iowa. I had the chance to make a three-minute statement, and I used it to concentrate on the fact that United States was probably the only country in the world that could give a first-generation immigrant like me the chance to serve at such a high-level federal government position. I stated that after Salina and I got married, we had forty-eight dollars to start our lives together. I would do everything I could to be a good US citizen and federal government officer. The senator from Iowa said that he knew that ISU wanted me to be their Dean of Agriculture, and I turned them down. I thought he was going to give me a hard time for that. Instead, he continued to state that he himself was a first-generation immigrant and welcomed me to serve the US federal government. There were questions from a couple of Senators from other states. Mostly, these Senators just wanted to make a statement to please their hometown folks. A couple of them left before we finished our answers to their questions. Nevertheless, the hearing lasted for over two hours.

Later that day, we were told that the committee had passed our nominations and sent them to the full Senate floor for a vote. The next day, the full Senate passed our nominations and sent them to the White House. President Bush signed the confirmation on July 10. Jim Mosley and I were sworn into our position on July 11, 2011.

Joseph became the under-Secretary of USDA on July 11, 2001 at Washington DC

CHAPTER 18
Managing the REE Programs

The job of the Under-Secretary of REE at USDA turned out to be a unique and powerful position than I expected. One significant showing of the position was that the Washington magazine, *Nations*, published once every two years an issue of the "Nation's Top 100" most influential persons. I was on the cover of the issue in 2002. My photo was near the center of the cover, just below the Secretary of State Colin Powell. The one hundred included government, industry, and NGO executives. Several cabinet members did not even make the list. In the issue, it had a brief description for each person on the cover. It stated that I was low profile but had significant contributions to the US government connections with China and Asian countries. I did represent US visiting China, Japan, India, Australia, Indonesia, and Malaysia.

The major duties of the position included the following: (1) managing the four major units within the USDA, which are the Agricultural Research Service (ARS), CSREES, Economic Research Service (ERS), and National Statistics Service (NASS); (2) representing USDA at congressional budget hearings and of matters related to REE operations at all federal government meetings related to science and technology; (3) being a member of the White House Office of Science and Technology (OSTP) committees; and (4) representing the US government as chief scientist of agriculture at international gatherings.

Although there were no official hours of my daily work, but it did not matter much, as I was on call by the Secretary of Agriculture and by the White House at all times. In general, I was at my office from 7:00 a.m. to 6:00 p.m., Monday to Friday. We worked half a day on Saturday and could take a day off on Sunday and holidays, if there were no urgent matters to take care of. I did not have the means to live in Washington, DC, so I bought a town house in Leisure World, a retirement community at Silver Spring, Maryland. The commute from my town house to the office was thirty minutes to two hours each way depending on the traffic. Therefore, I had long working hours.

Joseph on How2US cover November 2003 issue at Albany, CA, US

My office was on the second floor of the Whitman Building, on the National Mall, next to the Smithsonian Institute Building. It is the only federal government office on the Mall ground. The REE office was a seven-room cluster at one end of the main building facing the National Mall. When I first moved in the office, the layout of the office had my administrative assistant occupy the end room, next to a small conference room. My office was next to the conference room, then the office of two assistant staff, and the Deputy Under-Secretary's office. All these rooms had a view to the National Mall. Across from these rooms were three rooms for the REE budget director and for my two confidential assistants, appointed by the USDA White House Liaison Office. There was an allocation of funds for me to buy new furniture and other things for my office. I decided to move myself to the end conference room and change my original office into a large conference room and equipped it with audiovisual equipment where we could do teleconferences with the outside world. Outside the auditorium in the South Building, there was no such facility in the Whitman Building. The USDA staff told me that I could not do that renovation because the small conference room did not have enough footage for an Under-Secretary's office. I measured the size of the room and asked them to open a door between the administrative assistant office and the small conference room, making it one room. It would meet the criteria, and it was done. Thus, from my new office, I had a direct view of the Washington Monument through the window. Everyone who came into my office enjoyed the view.

Salina accompanied me to the move to DC. We bought the townhouse at Leisure World of Silver Spring in three hours. It turned out that it was the best investment that we ever did in our life. We sold it five years later for more than double the purchase price and made a good profit. The adult community had a club-house with activities, such as a computer class and Spanish language class that Salina could attend. The instructors were very good to Salina. So we donated our computer, printer, and accessories to the computer lab when we left DC. There was also a Maryland Senior Center not far from our place. On the days Salina wanted to go to the Senior Center, she would drop me off at the Silver Spring Metro subway station. There was a Metro station at the Smithsonian Institute with only a short walk to my office. Salina enjoyed the line dance class and woodwork class at the Senior Center and eventually volunteered to be the instructor of the Tai Chi class.

To protect my identity, she never mentioned my name. So one time, when I went to the Center with her, the staff called me, "Mr. Fond, nice for you to join us!"

Nevertheless, life was boring for Salina as we had few friends in DC.

Each Monday morning, the Secretary had her staff meeting in the morning to review matters on hand and make any assignments, if any. In the afternoon, I had my REE staff meeting with the four administrators, budget director, and my office staff. Besides passing on any important matters I learned in the morning session, each administrator would report any significant activities at their agency and any matters that needed direction from me.

One of the first things I did as the REE head was to use the leftover year-end discretion fund to purchase thirty-six DNA sequencing analyzers and placed them at different ARS laboratories. The staff were quite surprised of my action. It seemed that most others in my position in the past usually used the fund to take expensive vacations. My action brought praises from the Director of NSF, who was the chair of several committees of the OSTP. The director of OSTP was a staff of the president who saw the President daily and provided answers of science and technology matters to the President. The Director of NSF stated, "Wow, we finally have someone from USDA who is a real scientist and we can talk to!"

The second thing I did for ARS was to upgrade their research review system. ARS had a review system in place for years, but the review was performed by inter-nal reviewers. I required them to invite outside well-known scientists in the field of the research to review the performance by the researchers and receive a grade. The grade would be tied in with their annual salary increases. I also asked them to have economic impact statement so the projects were much easier to justify when it came to budget allocation. I even sat in a couple of the reviews that I was familiar with. All of a sudden, researchers had to write up detailed and well-thought-out research plans. Since ARS was supposed to perform long-term research, I asked them to do the review once every five years. The staff needed to turn in yearly reports. Lastly, I wanted ARS to support their researcher with enough funds so that each researcher could have enough funds to hire a postdoc, hire a technician, and purchase small equipment and supplies. I also asked CSREES to open up the ARI grants to ARS scientists to submit proposals to compete with the land-grant institutes and other scientists. We attracted many outstanding researchers from other academic institutes during my tenure, and I had met a number of them.

Growing A Nation plaque, one of Joseph's completed projects
at USDA, June 8, 2005, Washington, DC

One interesting small story was that without knowing it, I imitated President Abraham Lincoln on a speech I delivered for the ARS fiftieth anniversary celebration event. As Under-Secretary, I got many invitations to make addresses at various kind of meetings and conferences. Thus, I had six speechwriters; one from each of the four agencies for specific topics related to their areas of responsibilities, another one for international conferences, and one staff for making wonderful PowerPoint presentations. It was not uncommon that I was handed a speech write-up when I boarded a plane to deliver the speech at a particular conference or meeting. There were only two times that I can remember that I did not use any written scripts. Once was at an annual meeting of the Association of Public and Land-Grant Universities (APLU), and the other was at the ARS fiftieth anniversary event. There was not enough time for the ARS speechwriter to seek my inputs to craft a presentation. I wrote a few words on a piece of napkin on the airplane and delivered the speech and showed the audience the napkin. Apparently, when President Lincoln delivered his important Gettysburg speech, he did not use any script and spoke from a piece of napkin. All Americans knew about the story when they studied American history, except those of us not educated in US elementary and high schools. Therefore, the ARS audience must have thought that I tried to impress them by doing the same as what President Lincoln did. The good thing was that I must have gotten their devoted attention. A couple of research leaders came up to me after the meeting and said that they were glad that I spoke about bring back long-term basic science research into ARS laboratories. They said it was about time that a real scientist was the Under-Secretary of REE.

I also did seek chances to visit ARS laboratories. ARS had 106 research locations inside the US and 6 in foreign countries. Several locations never had an REE Under-Secretary visit them before. I recalled that once I was in Woodland, Oklahoma, the city folks told me that the last time a DC officer visited them was President Roosevelt. Another time, I was in Guam, and the governor was so happy that I visited. He assigned a security guard to follow me everywhere. The guide even stood outside my bedroom the whole night. I had never been treated like that before in my life, nor afterward.

The ERS had an important mission to produce research to review and forecast the economy of crops and livestock for the US and the world. However, they were underfunded and often could not pursue interesting projects due to a shortage of funds and proper personnel. During my tenure, I nearly doubled the budget for ERS. At the peak time, they had 250 economics PhDs under one roof, more than the rest of the federal government agencies added together. They developed an award-winning website that carried important economic news daily. When I was in Hungary for a visit, the Hungarian government Secretary of Commerce told me that the first thing he did when he arrived at the office was to check on the ERS website.

I also did visit CSREES and NAAS offices but not as often as to the ARS and ERS locations. CSREES had only five hundred or so staff, but most were senior scientists and functioned well over the years.

When I was with UGA, one of the outside activities I had was to be a member of a committee to propose a new competitive grant program called ARI, to be managed by CSREES. The thought was that most CSREES grants were fixed funding, distributed to the state AES and extension services, according to the Hatch and Smith Act. The new ARI program was open for researchers of all colleges to submit proposals. The competition was based on the merits of the peer review panels, much like the NIH grants that had been operating for years. The end report submitted to Congress in 1988 called for Congress to allocate $500 million new money to establish this program. The program was established by Congress in 1989 with less than $100 million, and it stayed at that level for ten years. When I became the REE Under-Secretary, I requested $200 million for ARI in my first-year budget proposal and received the support of the secretary. However, White House only requested $150 million, and Congress gave us $130 million for year 2002 budget. Eventually, when I left DC in 2005, the ARI fund had reached $170 million. Many people credited me with the creation of a competitive grant program in the USDA.

Once, when the OSTP committee on nanotechnology was setup, I could not find any ARS scientist who knew the field, so I appointed Dr. Hongda Chen of CSREES, who had a chemical engineering background, as the USDA representative. Hongda went on to become the Director of the nanotechnology program, which I allocated some special fund in the CSREES ARI program. He later became the most knowledgeable person in the subject matter in USDA and was the editor of several books on agricultural nanotechnology. People asked me how I knew Hongda would be so successful. My answer was that it was my instinct.

NASS actually had over one thousand staff because they had to do the Agricultural Census once every five years. They were so well trained in conducting census that when I was in China, their Bureau of Census requested that I send NASS staff to assist them to train their staff to do their national census.

In less than one year, I won the trust of all four-unit administrators and their staff. The REE operated smoothly, and I had a lot of fun managing a very challenging division of the USDA.

CHAPTER 19
Chairman Jiang

In November 2001, the Ministry of Science and Technology (MOST) of China held the first International Conference on Agricultural Science and Technology in Beijing and invited the Agriculture and Science and Technology Ministers of other countries to attend. As the chief scientist of USDA, I was sent to Beijing to represent the US. The conference attracted over thirty Ministers around the world to attend.

Since my last name is spelled J-E-N, which was not the normal spelling of the Chinese word *Ren* in China, MOST was not aware that I was a Chinese American. They provided me with a translator as my escort throughout the conference and a Merced car and a driver. Once my background was checked, the staff of MOST and other Ministries were excited. Several Ministries requested to have meetings with me outside the conference.

One of the activities at the Conference involved a visit with the Chinese President and the Communist Party Chairman Jiang Zemin at the Great Hall of the People. The visit was originally scheduled for fifteen minutes, as a courtesy to the limited number of foreign delegates and a few well-known scientists, both Chinese and global.

As we walked into the Great Hall of the People, there were four sofa seats next to the head table, two on each side, and three rows of seats on both sides. According to the Chinese custom, the right-side seats were reserved for the host, and the left-side seats were for the honored guests. The most honored guest of our group was Dr. Norm Borlaug, the father of Green Revolution and a Nobel Prize winner, who was seated next to the head table. I was told to sit next to him as the representative of all the foreign scientists. The right-side seats were for Chairman Jiang and the Minister of MOST, Dr. Hu Guanghua.

After we all seated for a while, Chairman Jiang walked into the hall with all of us standing and clapping. After the Minister of MOST made a short and general introduction, Chairman Jiang greeted us all and acknowledged the presence of Dr. Borlaug. Then he turned to me and asked, "You must be a Chinese? Do you speak Mandarin?"

I answered, "Yes, Mr. Chairman," in Mandarin.

He then asked me in Mandarin, "Where were you born?"

I answered in Mandarin, "Mr. Chairman, I was born in Chongqing."

He seemed to be surprised and then asked in the Sichuan dialect, "Do you speak Sichuan dialect?"

I responded in Sichuan dialect, "Yes, Mr. Chairman."

He asked, "Where did you grow up?"

I said, "In Shanghai and Nanjing area."

He looked surprised and asked in the Shanghai dialect, "When did you leave Shanghai?"

I replied in Shanghai dialect, "In 1949."

He smiled and said, "I see." He turned to the Minister of MOST and said, "You see, he left Shanghai in 1949 and can still speak Shanghai dialect. You were born in Shanghai, and you do not know how to speak Shanghai dialect."

Chairman Jiang seemed to be very excited to find someone who could speak the dialect he was most familiar with. He became quite talkative, using English and Mandarin toward the group but speaking in the Sichuan dialect or Shanghai dialect to me. The meeting ended up lasting for an hour and forty-five minutes. His staff was pacing outside the room like ants on a hot plate. I was sure he missed several other appointments because of the unexpected extended session with us.

During the meeting, the chairman stated that China now had two major problems. One was that the country not only produced enough grains to feed the people, but they had excess grain production to the point that they could not store all of them. Thus, some grains were being lost due to rats and mold growth. On the other hand, although the people had enough to eat, they did not eat enough proteins in their diets. The second major problem was that people were migrating to a few major cities at large numbers and creating problems in regard to city development and shortage of labor at the agricultural field and small villages. Then he turned toward me and asked, "What do you think we should do?"

I was surprised for a second but answered, "If you have excess grains but are short on storage spaces and people need more proteins, maybe you can consider developing the livestock industry." I continued, "In the northwest region of China, you are having real problems with soil erosion and desertation due to deforestation over the past two decades. Instead of replanting forest trees, which will take decades to grow, maybe you can encourage the growth of grassland, which can slow down the soil erosion on the one hand and develop the livestock industry, particularly dairy husbandry, on the other hand." After a pause, I continued, "As for the people's problem, there is no magic solution. I can offer a suggestion that can solve part of the problem. I suggest the development of food processing industry in second-tier cities at each province." I continued, "China has many local foods that can be exported to other countries or can be sold to other parts of China. Right now, when it comes to harvest time, many agricultural products are wasted due to lack of transportation and food preservation methods. Food processing can preserve these products. Besides, the development of food industry not only means the building of factories, one must first build infrastructures such as roads, electricity, and water supplies, and then maintain these facilities. Someone also needs to build supporting industries like tin plate canneries, label printing shops, bottling and packaging factories, and marketing and sales firms. It can attract quite a number of local people to work at these nearby second-tier cities instead of flooding to Beijing or Shanghai."

He listened carefully, and after I finished, he stared at me intensely for what felt like a long time. The entire Great Hall of the People became so silent that one could hear a pin drop. I was saying to myself, *How stupid of me! How can I talk like that!*

Then Chairman Jiang turned to the Minster of MOST and the Minster of MOA and said, "We have been thinking like that for a while, right?" All his staff nodded and agreed with him. I admired the quick wisdom of Chairman Jiang. He took my idea and turned it into his idea with a simple short question.

At the end of the meeting, Chairman Jiang greeted a few guests in sequence, and I was the last one. He held my hand for a long while and asked me about my life in the US. Finally, he said "You not only speak the language well, you have deep understanding of cultural practices of us and them. There are things only you can accomplish and very few other persons can. I hope you can come to visit China often."

I answered, "Thank you for your confidence. I will try to seek opportunities to do so."

The day after the meeting, the official Chinese newspaper *China People's Daily* printed a front-page article that "China will develop livestock and food processing industries!" The article noted that these were the instructions from Chairman Jiang.

Few years later, the MOST Deputy Minister Mr. Li Xueyong told me that the food processing industry developed so fast in China that the industry had become the leading light industry in China. The dairy industry also developed very fast in the inner Mongolia and other regions of China. It became world famous with the melamine incident in 2008. It is now the most regulated industry in China.

Even after I left USDA and returned to Cal Poly, Minister Hu Guanghua still hosted me for unofficial private meals when I visited Beijing. He also told me that Chairman Jiang often asked him about my situation in the US.

When I reflected on my five-year tenure as the Under-Secretary of USDA, that two-minute response to Chairman Jiang was probably the most influential two minutes in my life. It was unknown how the words had benefited the people's lives in China.

CHAPTER 20
A Liaison Person

Besides managing the four units in REE and if I were interested in staying in DC for political life, I would need to interact with congressional staff. However, I had no such interest and treated my stay at DC as a guest. To deal with congressional contacts, I hired two former congressional staff as my assistants. They had several years of experience as congressional staff before and, therefore, could handle the job well. Nevertheless, sometimes, some senator or congressman would call me directly and ask me questions or demand actions.

My first test came from the Minnesota (MN) Senator who called me to his office to discuss placing an ARS soybean genetic expert in his state. I guess he was answering to a soybean farmer's request from MN. To emphasize the meeting, he had the other MN Senator there as well.

After he made his request, I answered, "I am sorry I cannot do that."

He asked, "Why not?"

I said, "The Congress has mandated that the ARS can only have six soybean genetic experts, and all six have been placed in other states for many years."

He said, "I do not care how you do it, just do it!"

I said, "Mr. Senator, you can do one of two things: the first is to discuss with your colleagues who has an ARS genetic expert in their state to transfer the position from their state to MN. Or you can establish a new law and ask the Congress to add to ARS budget for a new soybean genetic expert to be placed in MN." I know he could not do either option. No other senator would agree to transfer the position from their state to MN. They had to face soybean farmers and the industry of their state. He also could not have a new law for this kind of project, otherwise, all Senators could have their own request of any experts in any field from USDA or other federal agencies.

The two senators looked at each other and said to me, "Thank you for coming to my office to discuss this matter. We will think about it and get back to you if we need you to act." I never heard from this Senator again.

My second call from Congress was from the congressman from North Dakota (ND). The Congressman from ND was the most powerful politician from that state. This was because each state had two senators, disregarding the population, while the number of congressmen was decided by the population. ND had a low population and thus had two Senators but only one Congressman. He asked me to go visit ARS locations in his state because he wanted to be sure that ND got their share of the ARS funding and scientists. We met at Grand Forks, ND, where one of the six ARS human nutrition units was located. This particular unit was a smaller unit, with specialization in legume research. The unit Director was very excited as no REE Under-Secretary had visited the unit before. He served a meal in which all dishes were made with various kinds of beans. He was very surprised to hear that I had extensive knowledge on legumes. This was due to my experience at UGA when we had a ten-year State Department and US Agency for International Development (USAID) contract to assist African countries to develop new products from their staple food, cowpeas, known to US as black-eyed peas. I told him some new ideas that he could try, to develop new products to assist the bean industry in the state and in US. The Congressman was very impressed and said that I really knew about nutrition. I told him that I used to teach Human Nutrition class at CU years ago.

We then moved onto Bismarck, ND, where an ARS unit was performing molecular biology research. The unit leader was very proud of all the new equipment they obtained. When one of his scientists told us that one equipment could determine the molecular weight of proteins, I corrected him that he meant peptides, and not proteins. The molecular weight of proteins was into the millions, and no equipment in the world could determine it yet. The scientist was red-faced and admitted that he was wrong. The Congressman was really impressed of my scientific knowledge. After the trip, he became one of my strong supporters for federal budget requests.

He told his colleagues, "We should leave Joe Jen alone to do his work. Joe really knows his field, and he even corrected my scientist at our ARI unit in ND." After that, there were few Senators and Congressmen who called me anymore.

The other major responsibility of being the chief scientist of USDA was to be a member of the OSTP Committees and Subcommittees. The Director of OSTP was a well-known physics professor from New York University who served as a member of the President's staff and saw the President daily. He provided the President with advice on science and technology-related questions. The OSTP Committees were to coordinate the budget and planning of science and technology projects. The actual works were carried out by the Subcommittees. There were originally three Committees: one on science, one on technology, and one on environment. A fourth Committee on national security was added after the 9/11 event. Most Committee and Subcommittee meetings were called quarterly by the OSTP Director, and I would attend them if I was in DC. I was the cochair of the Science Committee with the Director of NSF, who was a microbiologist from the University of Maryland (UM). The Director was very happy that I pushed for basic science emphasis in ARS research.

As a result of my management of USDA/REE and the OSTP work, I received a rare citation for leadership by the Council of Scientific Society Presidents (CSSP).

The CSSP had over 150 members who were Presidents of professional societies. This included science societies, such as physics, mathematics, chemistry, and biology; economic societies, such as accounting, business, and management; and social science societies, such as history, philosophy, etc. Each year, the Director of CSSP called for nomination of the leadership citation. Usually, there were thirty or more nominations.

Joseph received the CSSP citation of leadership award at Washington DC in October 2006

The first round of election resulted to ten or less nominees, and the second round of election resulted to three top nominees. The third-round ballot must result to one of the three finalists receiving more than half of all eligible votes. If the third ballot did not produce a winner, they would skip the year without any winner. Before me, the winners included the Chairman of the Congressional Committee of Science, the President of Princeton University, and others. I was the first person in the agricultural field to win the citation. It remained as the most treasured award in my life.

Besides the domestic activities, I also represented USDA and the US to attend international science exchange programs. I visited Japan, India, and China with the Director of OSTP. On behalf of USDA, I also visited China, Hungary, Malaysia, Indonesia, France, and United Kingdom.

During my tenure as Under-Secretary of USDA, I visited China nine times—more than any other cabinet level members in the Bush administration. I was treated extremely well by every Chinese officer I had ever met. Many of them would request meeting with me on each of my visits. The US Embassy driver once said to me, "Most other Secretaries come to Beijing for three or four days to attend one meeting. You attend three or four meetings every day when you are here." I was invited by former President Bush to attend the US-Sino Cultural Exchange Conference and served as the keynote and session chair of the agricultural science and technology session. The Conference was held in October 2006 in Beijing, China.

I guess most politicians in Beijing heard about the story of when Chairman Jiang and I were at the People's Great Hall. In one sense, I was a good liaison person.

Joseph with former President George H. Bush at US-Sino Relationship Conference. (Taken in June, 2006 at Beijing, China)

In 2004, MOST and USDA signed five cooperative projects during one sitting between me and Mr. Li Xueyong, the Deputy Minister of MOST. It was a historical event for having the most agreement signings during one sitting in China. Over the next four years, USDA had many interactions with MOST, MOA, and other Chinese Ministries. USDA had sent several teams of scientists to the northwest region of China to assist them on soil erosion prevention and grassland regeneration projects. In 2007, Mr. Li told me that over the last three years, the food processing industry started at less than 1 percent to become the largest light industry in China, occupying 22 percent share of all the light industries.

For one of my three trips to India, the Department of State requested me to meet with the Indian Department of Agriculture. The goal was to try to have them agree to the import of Bacillus thuringiensis (Bt) cotton seed from the US. With the humid weather of India, fungus growth was a major problem for traditional cotton seeds. Oftentimes, the cotton farmers would lose the whole crop to fungus infection. The Bt cotton seed was a GMO and was prohibited from being imported into India. I was told that for survival reason, some Indian cotton farmers bought Bt cotton seeds on the black market and had good success and bountiful harvest. However, if the Indian government found out about it, they would destroy the crop and ask the farmers to pay a fine. Some farmers could not pay the fine and committed suicide. When I met with the Indian Minister of Agriculture, he had over thirty of his assistants and management teams meet with me. After I presented the case to him, he was somewhat embarrassed that he did not know the real situation. It seemed that the US ambassador and his assistant tried but was not able to relay the scientific facts of the GMO cotton seeds to the Indian side. The Agriculture Minister told me that he would discuss the matter over with his staff and give me a reply. Less than one week later, the Indian government agreed to open the importation of the Bt cotton seeds from the US. Although my meeting helped the US cotton seed industry, I was happy that I probably saved a few farmers' lives in India.

Other times, the foreign Minister of Science and Technology or Agriculture would visit DC and had meetings with me. One such occasion was with the Minister of Science and Innovation from Malaysia. Agriculture and biology were part of his responsibilities, so he came to DC to sign cooperation agreement with me. He also invited me to attend his scientific conference in Malaysia, which I did once.

It could be said that I had a very busy schedule as the Under-Secretary of USDA/REE. Nevertheless, since I did not spend time to interact with Congressional activities, I had time to accomplish these projects that benefited the USDA and the citizens of the US and the world. That was the most satisfying part of my appointment.

Joseph was keynote speaker at Malay-US Science and Innovation
Conference at Kuala Lumpur, Malaysia in August, 2005

CHAPTER 21
Genomics and Obesity

If I could only use two words to express my tenure of the five years as Under-Secretary of USDA, it would be *genomics* and *obesity*. The former was a very successful story while the second one was not so.

When I first came on board, several animal science society leaders and lobbyists came to my office and asked if I could assist to fund the DNA sequencing of an animal. It was the year that the sequencing of the human genome and rice genome were to be completed. The Human Genome Project was headed by NIH, with fifteen international countries, and cost many millions of US dollars. They had been working on it for over ten years. The sequencing of the rice genome was led by NSF and several countries as well. USDA did participate in the rice project. I thought the proposed animal genome project was interesting and agreed to look into it. I visited the Director of the NIH Human Genome Institute and found that he was thinking of starting a project on comparative genome to sequence living things according to the development chart, from the amoeba to the monkey.

I said to him, "How about you help to sequence a cow as the example of mammals, a chicken as the example of birds, and a honeybee as the example of insects."

He thought that was not a bad idea but said that his institute could contribute half of the cost of the sequencing and asked me to assist him to find the other half of the funding. He was thinking I might be able to use USDA/REE funds or ask for new budgets from the Congress. The budget of USDA/REE was very tight, and there were too many other priorities for USDA to think about to ask for a new budget for the sequencing projects. I had different ideas on who to approach regarding the funding of the projects.

I first approached the livestock industries. They were very supportive, but most animal science societies did not have the means to contribute millions of US dollars. Only two industry groups did commit half a million dollars each. I then approached the international science community. The Canadian Gene Institute agreed to contribute $5 million while the Australia and New Zealand group each committed $1 million. USDA did not have extra funds to contribute. It happened that we got some additional allocation of ARI fund that year, so I directed $10 million toward the cow genome project.

ARS squeezed out one million from their allocation. I also directed the year-end half million toward the project. In the meanwhile, the cost of DNA sequencing had been decreased due to advanced technology. It was estimated that the cow genome project could be done with $100 million. Therefore, I was about $20 million short of the goal.

Also, I started to check into which agency could perform the DNA sequencing projects. There were four major sequencing centers in the US. The Department of Energy Center in San Jose was doing projects for their agency only, so it was not a target. Out of the three commercial sequencing centers, the center at Baylor Medical School located at Houston, TX and the one at Washington University Medical School at St. Louis, Missouri, were keen on bidding for the projects. Since I was at the USDA Human Nutrition Center at Baylor, I contacted the Baylor Center. The Director of the Baylor Center was very excited and showed me their seventy-seven sequencing machines. I learned that there was no need for high-powdered scientists to do the sequencing. It only needed trained technicians to run the machines and watch out for breakdowns.

While I was at Baylor, I received a phone call from a Mrs. McDonalds. She said to me that she heard that I needed some funds to complete the funding of the Cow Genome Project. I was not sure who she was and how she learned about the project. She went on to say that if I could be sure to assign the project to Baylor Center, she could ask the Texas governor to get me the needed money. I thanked her for her kindness, but all federal projects have to be open to bids by anyone, I could not guarantee that Baylor Center could win the bid.

She just said, "You will hear from the Texas Governor's Office soon."

Upon my return to DC, the personal assistant to the Texas governor did call and said what Mrs. McDonalds said to me. When I consulted with our in-house expert in this field, they all agreed that Baylor Center was the best place to conduct the project. With that, USDA sent out the project for bid, and Baylor Center did win the bid, and the project was started soon.

In addition, the honeybee project was first done by Baylor Center, as the size of the genome was very small, and the NIH Human Genome Institute used year-end fund to fund it. The chicken project was awarded to the Washington University Medical Center by NIH, as the Poultry Science Association approached NIH for assistance on the project. Since the size of the chicken genome is also small, NIH agreed to the project. USDA did assist both projects in providing technical assistance, and I did provide some donated funds to NIH on both projects.

Instead of taking several years to complete the project, Baylor Center stopped all other projects and concentrated on getting the Cow Genome Project done in eighteen months. We hosted a celebration event in the Whitten Building. Besides Secretary Ann Veneman, the Director of OSTP also showed up. He mentioned to the Secretary that "Your Joe is a doer!" He meant to say I could get things done under the most difficult conditions. The project won many appreciations from the animal science field and other scientific community. The *Science* magazine published a rare comment to praise my project and pay tribute to me.

A side story about the genome story was that a professor at Duke University contacted me about assisting to start a project in sequencing the DNA of the poplar trees. When asked why she contacted me, she said that everybody told her that I was Mr. Genomics in DC. She was the President of the Forestry Association and a professor at the Duke University School of Environment Science. Eventually, I did assist her to get the Department of Energy Center to do the sequencing, as the center was interested in environmental projects.

The whole genome sequencing (WGS) became very popular among all biological science fields. We knew at the time that if the cost of the sequencing could be lowered, many more uses could be developed. Our goal was to lower the cost to $1,000 per human genome. It was achieved in ten years after the Cow Genome Project, which was earlier than we anticipated by five years. In January 2018, the USCDC announced that fifty-one public health inspection laboratories of forty-six states had been equipped with WGS to monitor the outbreak surveillance of listeria. By the end of the year, all such laboratories in fifty states were equipped with WGS. In addition to listeria, WGS would be used to trace and monitor campylobacter, salmonella, STEC (Shiga toxin-producing *E. coli*), and shigella. Before WGS, CDC had used pulsed-field gel electrophoresis (PFGE) for the past twenty years. They had traced and identified foods like ice cream, frozen vegetables, and caramel apples as outbreak sources and made these foods safer for the consumers. This was an example where genomics research had benefitted consumer food safety.

Joseph received the appreciation plate from the USDA graduate school for his leadership of the General Administration board of the graduate school from 2001 to 2005. (Taken in April, 2005 at Washington, DC.)

When VP of China Academy of Sciences, Dr. Chen Tze, came to DC to sign a cooperative agreement with me between his Academy and USDA, he mentioned that he worries about the risky obesity problem with Chinese children. After he was done, I checked into the situation in the US and found that one in four in the US population was overweight or obese. Also, there was an alarming and increasing rate of obesity in young children in the US.

I mentioned this situation to the Director of OSTP and suggested that a subcommittee to study obesity be considered. He thought it was a good idea and told me to organize it. To gain support from other federal agencies, I decided to organize a National Obesity Prevention Conference. Most all federal agencies were very supportive, particularly the military groups. However, one agency that did not support it was the NIH. When asked why, the answer was that they already had four Obesity Research Centers working on developing drugs to treat obesity. I realized that if the obesity prevention worked, these research Centers would be out of business. Nevertheless, I thought it was wrong that they took their own interest ahead of the health and well-being of the American citizens and the world population. I went ahead and hosted the conference in DC. We reported the findings to the Director of OSTP, and eventually, a Subcommittee on Overweight and Obesity was formed without the word *prevention* to satisfy NIH. The Subcommittee was cochaired by Dr. Carid Rexroad of USDA/ARS and the Director of the obesity unit from NIH. It held scheduled meetings and did effective budget allocation in this area by most federal agencies. After I left DC and Dr. Carid Rexroad retired from ARS, no significant progress was made on obesity research. Thus, I felt that the project was not as successful as the genomic project.

CHAPTER 22
A Dream Garden

When I visited Sydney, Australia, I took a city tour that stopped at ten spots. One of the stops was a Chinese garden. It was a small garden of two acres in size, with one building, which sold Chinese teas and dim sums. Having been to many Chinese gardens in China, I thought to myself that this was not a typical Chinese garden. That was the birth of my idea of the Dream Garden.

When I went back to DC and had a chance to visit the national arboretum, a unit under the administration of ARS, I talked to the Director about the idea of building a classical Chinese garden at the arboretum. The Director was quite interested in the idea and took me to the center of the arboretum and showed me an area of roughly thirteen acres, which he thought could be an ideal spot for a Chinese garden. The arboretum was in the northeast region of DC, with over four hundred acres of land. It already had some gardens: herb garden, Mediterranean garden, Asian garden, and vegetable garden. None of them had a building. It also had a National Bonsai Museum on-site. As such, the arboretum had all the equipment needed to maintain garden grounds and nearly one hundred employees with a curator for trees. I surveyed the site and thought the Director was right; the site was a place suitable to build the Dream Garden.

In talking with some local Chinese Americans, I found out that some of them had been thinking about a Chinese garden in the DC area. However, the land cost in DC was so high that the idea was formidable. Some of them formed a group to support my idea of building the Chinese garden inside the arboretum. The leader of the group was Dr. William Tai, who had experience in building a small Chinese garden at the Missouri Botanical Garden in St. Louis, Missouri.

When the Chinese ambassador to the US, Mr. Yang Jiechi, invited me to a dinner at his residence, I raised such an idea to him. I also prepared a two-page proposal to outline the idea and showed the location inside the arboretum. It turned out that the ambassador's wife was very familiar with the arboretum. She often took visitors from China to visit the arboretum for the famous azalea hill, the colony column, and the Bonsai Museum. Luckily, Mr. Yang was due to return to China for the annual report soon. He pocketed my proposal and went to see Ms. Jiang Zhewei, the party chief of Ministry of Forestry, who administrated gardens and environment. That was the summer of 2013.

In October 2013, Ms. Jiang visited Canada for a conference, and she extended her visit to come to DC to visit me and see the proposed site at the arboretum. She was so overwhelmed by the location and thought that there was no place on earth more suitable to build a great Chinese garden. She wanted to sign a letter of intent for China and the US to cooperatively build a Chinese garden at the site identified by the Director of the arboretum. The letter of intent was signed by Ms. Jiang and I.

In the spring of 2014, at the invitation of Ms. Jiang, I took the Director and curator of the arboretum and the chief engineer in charge of building and construction of all ARS unit to visit Yangzhou and Suzhou, where the best Chinese gardens were located. It happened that the husband of Ms. Jiang was a well-known garden designer. Mr. Peng was very enthusiastic of the idea that he started working on the design of the garden without seeing the site. The visit caused much enthusiasm in the local government and business, which I believe benefited Ms. Jiang in her fund-raising effort for the garden.

In the fall of 2014, Ms. Jiang visited DC again. We decided to attempt to build the garden. A memorandum of agreement (MOA) was signed by Secretary Veneman, Ambassador Yang, Madam Jiang and I. The MOA stipulated that the Chinese side was to provide all materials and labor needed to build the buildings and other structures, the plants, and the artwork for the buildings. The US side was to provide the land, the underground utility works, and the maintenance of the garden.

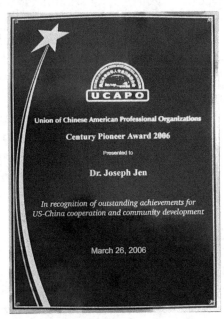

Joseph received the first ever Century Pioneer Award from the Union of Chinese American Professionals on March 26, 2006, Washington, DC, US.

I made a CD entitled, "Classical Chinese Garden at the National Arboretum." It outlined the thoughts of how the four elements of the Chinese garden—the water, the buildings, the plants, and the art furnishings—were necessary in the building of the garden. It showed the conceptual design developed by Mr. Peng. I commissioned a model of the garden be made using donated fund.

What took place afterward was beyond my imagination. I thought it was a simple project and never dreamed of running into so many obstacles and barriers.

First of all, the proposed garden needed to have approval from the Fine Arts Commission of the DC city government and the City Planning Committee. Furthermore, the US Congress learned about the news from the media and informed us that such an action must have the approval of the US Congress. Another group formed a Classical Chinese Garden Foundation. The Union of the Chinese American Professional Organization honored me with their first ever "Century Pioneer" award at their annual meeting held at McLean, VA. On March 26, 2006. It ended up that the DC Chinese Americans did not contribute greatly into the fund generation. Some of my personal friends and industry owners did become what I called pioneer donor by donating ten thousand dollars each.

After a couple of years, we first obtained the approval of the DC city government. With the assistance of Ambassador Yang, we got the US Congress to put in a supporting paragraph in the 2005 Farm Bill to allow the garden to be built. I was successful in putting in $8 million, the cost estimate of USDA's share to construct the garden site, into the President's budget for 2006. A real surprise took place at the 2006 congressional budget hearing. A young senator Obama from Illinois showed up at the hearing and opposed the garden project. He thought that if the National Arboretum were to build a world-class garden, why not build an English garden or a Japanese garden, which he thought was more famous than the classical Chinese garden. Congress had problem passing the budget that year and ended up using the continuing resolution to fund USDA budget. Continuing resolution meant Congress would provide the same amount of fund to USDA as in 2005. Therefore, none of the new projects for 2006 were approved. Thus, the $8 million for the Chinese garden was not allowed. After I left DC in 2006, the garden budget was never put back into the USDA budget request again. The project was on hold at USDA, even with the repeated requests by the Chinese government. For example, when Chinese president Hu Jintao visited DC, he requested to view the Chinese garden model. Then Secretary of State Hillary Clinton was his host. She asked the ARS to move the model to her office, and it was viewed by President Hu and Vice President Joe Biden. Ms. Clinton even agreed to move about $1 million of leftover fund from the World Expo held in Shanghai to be used to continue the architecture design of the garden. With Clinton's support, the project was extended and signed by then USDA Secretary Michael Nelson and the Chinese Ambassador Zhou Wenchong. However, the project was moved out of the REE control and placed under the Foreign Agricultural

Service (FAS) at USDA. It was a good move by the Agricultural Secretary at the time because the wife of the FAS administrator was Chinese. Unfortunately, the administrator left his job after two years, and the project had no owner and supporter at USDA anymore.

As time went on, Ms. Jiang was getting old, and after Mr. Peng died, she really wanted to have the garden built. She decided to pay for all the cost of building the garden instead of waiting for USDA to raise funds to pay for their share. She asked President Xi Jinping to assist. In late 2017, at the G20 meeting held in Hangzhou, China, President Xi approached US President Obama with the idea that the people of China wanted to give a classical Chinese garden as a gift to the American people. Obama could not find a reason to object to such an idea. Besides, he probably did not remember that he objected to the garden idea several years ago. When President Obama agreed to accept the gift, President Xi told him that he had already selected a date based on the Chinese farm calendar, and the project should start on October 29, 2017. On that date, a groundbreaking ceremony was held at the arboretum. A cornerstone was set down at the proposed garden site. I was invited to attend because Ms. Jiang insisted so. The construction of the garden had not started yet since the Chinese and American building codes were different. For the safety of onlookers, the American building codes needed the Chinese to change some parts of the design. I was told that the two sides were working to redesign part of the garden bit by bit. There was no telling when the garden would be completed.

SECTION 4

FOOD SAFETY

CHAPTER 23
Life After DC

My first international trip after leaving DC office was as the keynote speaker at the US-China Business Matching Conference held at Chengdu Sichuan, China in early August.

Joseph was keynote speaker at US-China Business Matchmaking Confidence 2006 in August, 2006 at Chengdu, Sichuan, China

When I left DC in May 2006, I returned to Cal Poly to be the special assistant to President Warren Baker as well as the special assistant to the CSU chancellor. My responsibility to Cal Poly was to be a liaison for the international programs. I took President Baker and other faculty members of Cal Poly to visit China Agricultural University (CAU), Nanjing Agricultural University (NJAU), Northwest Agriculture and Forestry Science and Technology University (NWAFSTU), Shanghai Jiao Tong University (SJTU), and Zhejiang University (ZU) in China. President Baker and Dean of Agriculture Dr. Dave Werner signed a number of cooperative agreements with these universities. We also established a dual master's degree programs with SJTU in dairy technology and a dual master's degree in forestry and range science with CAU. We had faculty and student exchange programs with CAU, NWAFSTU, and NJAU. Besides China, I also assisted Cal Poly to have cooperative and exchange programs with universities in Hungary and Mexico. These programs assisted Cal Poly to be lifted from the bottom of the CSU campuses in international programs into a more diversified international program.

My second trip after leaving DC was to Shanghai to visit the SJTU. They appointed me as the chairman of the advisory council of the new Bor S. Luh Food Safety Research Center. That appointment started my work on food safety for the following ten-plus years.

Later that year, I took the president and Mrs. Baker to visit SJTU in Shanghai and ZU in Hangzhou. The SJTU rolled out a red carpet to welcome the Bakers. They had a good time in Shanghai. In Hangzhou, the Deputy VP in charge of international program of ZU hosted us. President Baker wanted to visit their Energy Research Center, and the VP said okay. Arrangements for me and the president to visit the center was made. The center Director showed us a video (in Chinese) to introduce the Center. The Center had over three hundred doctorial researchers and five hundred graduate students. They had several pilot plants of various size. One of which was a semicommercial-scale pilot plant. President Baker was totally overwhelmed by the setups. However, everything they showed were in Chinese. President Baker asked if they had any English materials to share with him. The answer was that the Center was an internal institute, and for security reason, they were not open to any foreign visitors. President Baker then asked if they could share the video with him. They said they would consider it but never sent it to him.

One year later, I took president Baker and Dean Dave Werner to visit CAU in Beijing, NWAFSTU, at Yangling near Xian, and the NJAU in Nanjing. In Beijing, President Baker signed a Cal Poly agreement with CAU to establish a dual master's degree in forestry science and range management. At NWAFSU, Dean Werner signed an agreement to establish a faculty and student exchange program with their AGB program. At NJAU, we visited the Meat Science Center, which was considered to be the best in China. The Center Director took us to visit one of the largest meat science processing company in China. Their display cases had over one hundred meat items. Any Western breakfast meat items could be seen. President Baker and Dean Werner were surprised at the advanced equipment and food safety programs at the Meat Science Center and the meat processing company.

For the CSU chancellor, I was to be the liaison between the Chancellor's Office and the California agricultural industries. I developed a new Agricultural Advisory Council for the chancellor. The council was loaded with large California food and agricultural industry CEOs and directors. We met twice a year at the CSU system headquarters office at Long Beach, California. Besides the chancellor and his staff, the Presidents of all four CSU campuses with agricultural programs (San Luis Obispo, Fresno, Pomona, and Chico) all attended the meetings. The program was so successful that the President of the Eureka campus, which had a strong forestry program, and that of the Monterey campus, which had a strong marine science program, requested to participate as nonvoting members of the Council.

When I was the Under-Secretary of USDA/REE, I wanted to do something for Cal Poly. With the cooperation of Congressman Gary Dixon, who was on the CAL trip to China and Mongolia with me back in 1996, we crafted a Cal Poly ARI program much like the CSREES ARI program. It was not approved by the US Congress on Gary's first try. However, Gary was able to obtain the $1 million for Cal Poly ARI in the following farm bill.

Also, I proposed a California ARI program. The idea was to develop a granting fund for the four CSU campuses with agricultural program to compete for the California government grants of up to $4 million each year. Half of the funds were to be donated by the California agricultural industry to match the California government grants. Any campus that was not able to obtain the industry-matching fund, the remaining allocations to that campus's grant would be available for any CSU campuses to apply. These should be new money outside the regular CSU budget allocations from the California government. With the assistance of supporters in the California agricultural industries, we were successful to obtain $1 million to start the program in 2007. An Executive Director was hired from outside the CSU system to handle the competitive grant fund. The Director was stationed at the Fresno campus for the first five years. To simplify handling details, the $1 million for the Cal Poly ARI was lumped into the CSU ARI. The California ARI got increased to $2 million in two years. The Executive Director had a strong independent spirit and did not get along with the Fresno campus Dean of Agriculture well. So he resigned the post, and to save management fund, the position was assigned to Dr. Mark Shelton, the Associate Dean of graduate studies at Cal Poly. We eventually got $5 million grant from the California state government. Mark Shelton did a good job of handling the fund program over the years. The job gave him the chance to meet many Cal Poly alumni and California agricultural industry executives. I believe he enjoyed the chance to work on this program.

I was happy that I was able to assist both the Cal Poly and the CSU system to gain better reputations and new funding.

CHAPTER 24

International Forum on Food Safety

One of the areas that received my attention when I was the Under-Secretary of USDA was food safety. I provided increased funding in the competitive ARI grants to food safety. I also asked ARI scientists to work with CDC and FDA scientists cooperatively on annual strategic research planning conference. I also asked the CSREES and ERS to join in the conference. Eventually, USDA took the lead to establish the www.foodsafety.gov website located at the National Agricultural Library (NAL) site to serve as an authoritative resource. Educational institutes, media, and consumers could check and learn about food safety with the latest developments in the field.

A year before my retirement from USDA, my old neighbor in Taiwan Larry Li contacted me and asked me to assist a new Bor S. Luh Food Safety Research Center (Luh Center) established at SJTU in China. I told him I could not do anything while I was the "Under-Secretary of USDA." However, I planned to retire in 2006, and after that, I would be happy to assist. Dr. Luh was an old friend and colleague of mine in food science and technology field. On August 2016, shortly after my retirement, I was invited to make a food safety presentation at the SJTU.

The center was established in 2005, with a donation from the family of Dr. Luh, who worked at UC Davis for many years. He was an alumnus of SJTU, and in his will, he made a sizable donation to SJTU to set up the Luh Center. Larry Li was to oversee the donated fund deposited at the SJTU foundation. SJTU agreed to match the foundation donation, which could only be used for Center activities. Larry hoped that I could provide scientific and management advice to the Luh Center.

The next day of my visit to SJTU, they had a celebration at the Luh Center and invited me to attend. To my surprise, the short celebration was attended by VP Lin of SJTU, Dean Tang of the College of Agriculture and Biology, and Center Executive Director Dr. Shi Xianming. They asked me to make a short presentation about Dr. Luh and the interactions I had with him during the 1970s and 1980s. After the presentation, VP Lin came to the podium and announced that SJTU would form an Advisory Council for the Luh Center. He appointed me as the Chairperson of the council. Together with me, they also named five other people as members of the Council; two of whom were high-level officers of the Shanghai city government, two of them were director-level officers from the central government in Beijing, and one adviser was the CEO of a large dairy company in Shanghai. Under the circumstance, I did not have time to think of any reason to decline the appointment. We had a short advisory meeting the next day with only the two Shanghai officers in attendance.

I put some thought into the future of the Center and decided that to make the training of food safety and international conference as the short-term goal of the Center's strategic plan. The first three years, the Center's activities were concentrated in conducting the three International Symposia on food safety. In the meanwhile, I expanded the Advisory Council membership to include industrial and academic experts. From the industry, we added Dr. Chen Zemin, the owner of the Sanchuan, the largest frozen food company in China. From the academia, we added Dr. Yaowen Huang of UGA, who had expertise in HACCP trainings. I also asked Ms. Meng Suhe, who was the president of the Chinese Institute of Food Science and Technology (CIFST), to join us.

We approached industries for donations to start a goodwill food safety training course without charging any tuition to the participants. Seven companies answered our call. The first training course was held in 2007 at the Huashan campus of SJTU in Shanghai. In later years, when Dr. Zhou Pei, Party Chief of the College of Agriculture and Biology, became the Director of the Center, he had a strong support spirit of the Center. He hired Dr. Yue Jin from Canada as the Executive Director of the Center. Dr. Yue hired two full-time staff to handle the training courses.

Joseph was the keynote speaker at the GFSI (Global Food Safety Initiative) Focus Day China in August 2016 at Beijing, China

The training courses attracted international sponsors like the Global Food Safety Initiative (GFSI), the World Bank, and the US Grocery Manufacture Association (GMA) to be sponsors of the training courses. The result was that SJTU had become the authoritative entity for food safety training in China. Whenever the Luh Center announced a training course on their website, registrations would be filled within two or three days, with many on the waiting list. By 2020, the Luh Center had trained over one thousand trainees, and these trainees served as a rich source for information gathering for surveys the Center might conduct on subjects related to food safety, nutrition, and health. This was probably the most successful part of the Luh Center's activities.

The International Symposium of food science was a challenge as there was no funding source in SJTU to support such activities. The 2007 Symposium hosted by Dr. Shi Xianming was a huge success. Dr. Shi used his personal connections in the Shanghai city government to obtain a large contribution, and the city government served as cohost to the Symposium. Dr. Shi invited Frank Busta and Dave Lineback, both well-known food safety experts in the food microbiology and food safety field, to be speaker at the Symposium. However, the most attractive speaker was Dr. Robert Brackett, who was the Director of Food Science and Applied Nutrition (FSAN) of the US FDA. Dr. Brackett was an associate professor at UGA Griffin campus when I was the Division Chair there. He had a problem with being promoted to the full professor rank due to the blocking of older professors at the Athens campus. I assisted him to be promoted to full professor, and thus, he owed me a favor. His participation attracted several Chinese high-ranked officers from Beijing. It seemed that these officials had tried to invite Brackett to visit Beijing but was unsuccessful. They were totally surprised that Brackett would come to Shanghai for the Luh Center Symposium. The Symposium was held at the five-star Huating Hotel in Shanghai.

The second Symposium in 2008 was hosted by Dr. Dabing Zhang, professor of the College of Life Science and a Deputy Director of the Luh Center. Dr. Zhang was a well-known professor in GMO analysis research in China and was known worldwide. The symposium was held on SJTU main campus in Minghong District, just outside of Shanghai. The main campus had a good facility for conferences in terms of meeting facilities, printing, meal service, and other services. However, Minghong was still a new development district at the time and did not have five-star hotels. Most participants were able to stay at the housing facility of the campus's continuing education facility. The main campus did have a unique restaurant that was moved from Tokyo, Japan. The VIPs had meals at this special restaurant. Dr. Zhang had a number of his coworkers from Europe make presentation at the Symposium. This time, I got Dr. Merle Pierson, who was deputy Under-Secretary of USDA/REE, to participate. Merle was deputy Under-Secretary of USDA Food Safety for three years and due to return to Virginia Tech. At that time, my deputy Under-Secretary

Rod Brown left USDA to return to Utah State. So I invited Merle to be the deputy Under-Secretary of USDA REE to extend his stay in DC. Merle's presence also attracted many high-ranking central government officers from Beijing. These officers tried to pursue me to move the Symposium from Shanghai to Beijing so as to attract more government agency participations.

The 2009 Symposium was also a special session of the Fourteenth IUFoST Congress held at Hangzhou, a tourist city not far from Shanghai. This special session was held on the SJTU main campus hosted by Dr. Shaohui Zhang, who obtained his PhD from Japan. He invited his old adviser and other Japanese speakers to the symposium. Merle Pierson attended the IUFoST symposium in Hangzhou and thus was able to be at the special session as well. The good thing about having the Symposium at Minghong campus was that we had many students who participated as volunteers, and they could attend the symposium. The students came not only from the food science and engineering department but from all over the campus. It helped to attract more students to transfer into the food science major as well.

During a 2009 food safety conference sponsored by IUFoST and FIA China in Shanghai, I met Dr. Geoffrey Campbell-Platt of UK, the editor of an international scientific journal, *Food Control.* After the conference, the CIFST asked me to be in Beijing.

Joseph received the first ever Scientific Spirit Award from CIFST
and IUFoST on April 20, 2014 at Beijing, China

The CIFST and IUFoST were interested in sponsoring the International Forum on Food Safety. They needed to have Chinese central government support of such an activity. I agreed to assist them and contacted Dr. Chen Tze, the Minister of Health, who agreed to meet with us. He was quite interested in the proposal because the infant formula contaminated with melamine in China received global attention. Although Dr. Chen was not able to meet with us due to an emergency trip out of the country, he asked his deputy minister and several staff meet with us. The ministry of health agreed to be the major sponsor of the forum. Thus, CIFST and IUFoST were able to plan the first forum, which was held in April 2010, at the Friendship Hotel in Beijing. IUFoST was able to bring in WHO, FAO, the US IFT as cosponsors and supplied half a dozen foreign scientists who were specialist in food safety as speakers. CIFST obtained the strong support of Dr. Junshi Chen, the chief scientist of Ministry of Health and the eldest and best-known scientist in nutrition and food science in China. I assisted them by inviting high-level industry leaders from Cargill and McDonald's, as well as officers from USDA and USFDA. The forum was hugely successful, with over four hundred participants and nearly one hundred personnel from outside of China. It received major media coverage, including from the official newspaper *China Daily*. To give strong support to the forum, Dr. Chen Tze personally attended the forum and gave the opening remarks for the 2010, 2011, and 2012 forums.

I could not recall if any government officer attended the 2013 forum. That year, the central government formed the new China Food and Drug Administration (CFDA), more or less mimicking the USFDA. The CFDA was an independent committee equal in status to a Ministry. The Administration of Food Safety was transferred from MOH to CFDA. However, MOA still managed the food safety program of production agriculture. A new national food safety risk assessment center (CFSA) was formed under MOH. In the meanwhile, Dr. Chen Tze was promoted to be one of several Vice Chairmen of the People's Council (sort of like the US Congress), where laws and regulations were established. I visited the CFDA in January 10, 2014. The Vice Minister of CFDA, Mr. Teng Jiacai, the highest-ranked officer in charge of handling food safety matters, received me and four CIFST staff. He attended the 2014 and 2015 forum and gave the opening remarks at the opening sessions. In 2013 or 2014, CFSA became the third sponsor of the forum besides CIFST and IUFoST. A major rearrangement took place in 2017. The CFDA was deleted. I recalled that MOH was moved as part of a new committee on Planned Parenthood and Health. CFDA was changed into managing drugs only. No one seemed to be in charge of food safety during part of 2018, until a big State Administration for Market Regulation was formed. Food safety became a division of this inspection agency. The Director of food safety of this agency and the new Director of CFSA gave the opening remarks at the 2019 forum.

With the diminishing support of the central government on food safety, the support from IUFoST was lessened as well. With all these changes, the forum kept on going year after year due to the effort of Shao Wei, Chen Zheng, and other staff of CIFST. In 2018, the name of the forum was changed to the International Forum of Food Safety and Health to take in Chinese consumer interests in nutrition and health. With fewer foreign speakers from IUFoST, CIFST turned to domestic and Asian countries for speakers. I continued to assist CIFST and the forum as much as I could. In 2017, we started a new session to have high-level food industry CEO or directors interact with audience on food safety question with me being the monitor of the sessions, and it was very successful. It continued in the 2018 and 2019 forum.

In 2020, the planning of the forum was started in January, but everything was put on hold due to the coronavirus situation. China was on lockdown, and foreigners were not able to travel to China for meetings. Even after the lockdown was lifted, the Chinese central government had issued guidelines to encourage visual conference via Internet instead of large group gatherings in a big room. The 2020 forum was canceled. The forum might resume in 2021 and might be conducted web-based and in a small group in Beijing. I was sure, with the dedication of the CIFST staff, the forum would go on to serve its purposes till the need is gone. I wish the CIFST the best of luck, and I am confident the CIFST staff will continue the spirit of the forum for years to come.

During the more than ten years of time with the forum, I met a great many wonderful people from China and the rest of the world. It was a most satisfying experience in my life.

CHAPTER 25
Food Control Experience

In 2009, after our meeting with the Ministry of Health, Geoffrey asked me if I would be interested in being an editor for *Food Control*, an international journal with emphasis on food process control and food safety. It was also the official journal of IUFoST and EUFoST. After learning more about it and knowing that everything related to the editing would be handled online at any time and any place of my choice, I agreed to the suggestion. So on January 1, 2010, I became the second editor of *Food Control*. Geoffrey became the editor in chief of the journal, with a staff assistant located in Reading, UK. I was the editor to handle submissions from North America and Asian countries. Geoffrey would handle submissions from the rest of the world. We met once a year in Reading, UK, for the editor and publisher meeting at Geoffrey's home.

When I first joined *Food Control*, the impact factor of the journal was less than 2.0. By 2018, the impact factor was raised to 4.284, higher than *Food Microbiology, International Journal of Food Microbiology*, and *Journal of Agricultural and Food Chemistry*. The later was considered as the gold standard of all scientific journals in the food science and technology field. In 2010, we had 800 submissions, while in 2018, we had over 3,500 submissions. With the increased submissions, we decided, in 2005, that we needed to add an editor (Ralf Griener) to handle the Europe and South American submissions. With the vast increases in submissions from Asian countries, we decided to add another editor (Weibao Zhou from Singapore) in 2017. In 2019, we had over 3,700 submissions. On February 1, 2019, we added a fifth editor (Lihan Huang) to assist the handling of submissions from North America. Even with the addition of these editors, my workload of over eight hundred papers per year had maintained over the years.

With over ten years of experience on editing submissions to *Food Control*, I developed a presentation on how to publish articles in English-language international journals. It became a very popular presentation at various universities in China. By 2018, close to 45 percent of all *Food Control* submissions were from China. This was due to the Chinese system of awarding published papers, based solely on impact factors. For example, the *Journal of Food Protection* and the *Journal of Food Science*, the two journals who would review food safety papers, had an impact factor of around 1.5. Therefore, based on the Chinese award system, publishing one paper on *Food Control* would equal to publishing three papers in these two journals. The Western world did not understand or use this system. The troublesome matter to us editors at *Food Control* was that many submissions from China were not in the coverage areas of *Food Control*. However, the Chinese authors still tried to submit their paper to *Food Control*. It took a lot of editorial time and effort to process the rejection decisions on these submitted papers.

The year 2020 marked the thirtieth anniversary of *Food Control* since its inception in 1990. The editors and publisher decided to have a celebration activity by organizing a special session at the 2020 World Congress of IUFoST to be held in Auckland, NZ, in August 2020. The original idea was to have the five editors each contribute a presentation and to invite specific authors to contribute presentations. These selected papers would form the base of a special issue of *Food Control*. The program committee of the 2020 World Congress had a policy that all sessions had to be open to any author to submit papers. We had a very strong response on the special session that the program committee granted a rare doubt sessions to our proposal. We had to select from over thirty submissions from all over the world for the second session of five authors and left out many good papers without a chance to be presented at Auckland. Fortunately, the Congress would have poster sessions for these authors to participate, and they could submit their full paper for review for the special issue in *Food Control*.

Joseph was named as a Fellow of the International Union of Food Science and Technology on August 28, 2010 at the Cape Town, South Africa Congress.

To handle over eight hundred papers a year meant that I needed to handle between seventy to eighty papers a month. Besides reviewing the original submissions for suitable coverage in *Food Control*, for every paper accepted to review, I needed to find two or three qualified reviewers. Good reviewers are usually busy scientists and normally do not accept many review assignments. Some papers have to go through ten or more invitations before two reviewers were accepted to do the review. The normal review time for most reviewers is between three to twelve weeks. Once the reviews are collected, I have to make a decision whether to ask the authors to revise their paper or to reject their submissions. It was rare that a paper receive acceptance recommendation from the first round of review. There are always the difference of opinions of scientists. Most authors will take up to three months to revise their paper. Once they submit their revision, I can accept the revised paper without further review. Most of the time, the papers have to be reviewed twice or three times before I accept the paper for publication. The accepted paper would go to publishing manager for handling. Oftentimes, accepted papers can appear in an online version within two weeks for other scientists to read on the *Food Control* website.

For regular editors, these tasks would take fifty to sixty hours per week to handle the workload. I had two major advantages than normal editors in that I had an extensive network of good scientist, and my background covered all areas of agriculture, food chemistry, food microbiology, food safety, regulations and management. I also can make decisions quickly during the whole editing process. Nevertheless, it will still take me fifteen to twenty-five hours per work in front of the computer to complete my weekly assignments. Oftentimes, when I cannot sleep at night, it was the best time to work on editing. It was quiet, and the Internet was fast.

After over ten years of editing *Food Control*, the journal reached a very high rating in the food science and technology field, and it seemed time to think of terminating this task and start something new. It happened that the publisher informed us at the 2019 meeting in Reading that Elsevier had a new policy for each editor to stay for ten years. I decided to inform the publisher that 2020 would be my last year of involvement with the journal. It would have to take two or three new editors to handle the load I have carried. Nevertheless, life has to go on. The publisher explained that *Food Control* was now the flagship journal in the food science and technology field for Elsevier. She wanted to make sure that the journal would continue to have the kind of success as it has been in the past. After some thoughts, I recommended Dr. Hyun-GyunYuk from South Korea and Dr. Qinchun Rao from Florida State University to be the journal's new editors. Everyone agreed to the recommendations, and both of them were on board in April and June 2020. We discussed the need to hire a new editor to relieve the workload of Ralf Griener. Ralf recommended a scientist from Brazil who agreed to be on board by January 1, 2021. We further decided that we need a new editor in the consumer sciences. I recommended Dr. Bai Li from China and we all agreed and she will be on board in early 2021.

It has been an enjoyable and meaningful experience for me to be involved with *Food Control*.

CHAPTER 26
A Tale of Two Books

With the intense involvement of food safety issues in China from 2006 to 2016, I realized that food safety is a subject that not only involved science and technology, it also involve government laws and regulation, industrial managements, media reports, and social behaviors of the consumers. I thought of writing a comprehensive book to cover the whole area of food safety but knew I could not do it as I lacked expertise in many of the areas. Therefore, I looked into the possibility of editing such a book.

Once I decided to edit the books on food safety in China, I started to write down the different chapters and linked some of the experts in the fields as potential authors. I first divided the books into four sections: science and technology, laws and regulations, industrial management, and other topics, such as international trades. The science and technology section would concentrate on food microbiology, food chemistry, and new technology. The industrial management sections would contain various commodities.

Very quickly, I realized that the two areas that I needed assistance the most were the government laws and regulations and the analysis of risk management. Also, I did not know many Chinese experts in some of the fields. Luckily for me, I met Dr. Junshi Chen at the IUFoST World Congress at Monterey, CA, in September 2014. Dr. Chen is the best-known food science and nutrition expert in China. He is the first academician in the food and nutrition field in China. I talked to him about my concept of the books and asked if he would be interested in being a co-editor with me. He seemed to be interested in the idea. In the following months, we discussed the details of the book. The further we discussed the book, the more interested Dr. Chen became, and he participated actively on the planning of the book. We initially chose thirty chapters and divided them into six sections: introduction, food microbiology, food chemistry, laws and regulations, commodities, and new technology. Dr. Chen suggested that we added risk management as a new section due to the interest of the Chinese government on the topic. We eventually decided on seven sections and thirty-four chapters.

Joseph and his two books on Food Safety in China at Las Vegas, in March, 2017

During the months of November and December 2014, we started to send out invitations to potential chapter authors. Luckily, most of the invited authors accepted the writing assignments in a tight time schedule. We planned to complete the first draft of the book by the end of June 2015. All the chapter authors did manage to turn in their first draft in time except one. Thus, the book ended up with thirty-three chapters. Most of the authors were from China, but we did have several authors from outside of China. For those chapters, they were written in English and translated into Chinese.

What I did not know at the time was the fact that publishing books in China was a costly project. The publishers required us to pay the full cost of printing the books before they would start to process the book. I contacted the publishing department of SJTU and CAU and found the cost of publishing our book was at 50,000 to 70,000 RMB. Adding the translation, editing, designing of the book cover, promoting and, spending on other expenses, it was estimated that it might need a total of 200,000 RMB to publish the book. So I contacted my best friend in China, Mr. Chen Zeming, and a relative of mine in Hong Kong. They both agreed to make unconditional donations of 100,000 RMB each so we could publish the book.

Luck seemed to follow me in this event. I met an old friend, Dr. Chen Zhanglian, who used to be the President of CAU. He became the Deputy Governor of Guangxi Province for five years and returned to Beijing to become the Deputy Party Chief of the China Science Council. When he learned of my book idea, he indicated that his department had funds to support printing scientific books if the China Science and Technology Press could be the publisher. The press was a department of the China Science Council. He gathered the president and the chief editor of the press to meet with me and indicated to them that China science council would pay for the cost of publishing the book. His support also made the dealing with the editorial staff of the press easy for me and Dr. Chen. One of the ideas I had was that I wanted the book to be inexpensive so that many people, including the students, could buy a copy. Eventually, Dr. Chen and I signed a contract with the Press that we would not receive any royalty for the book so the book could be priced at 80 RMB per copy, less than the cost of a good meal at a good restaurant in Beijing.

Dr. Chen and I worked with the staff of the Press and started the editing and typesetting of the chapters on a rotating basis. In other words, the press would edit and typeset the chapters as the authors turned in their final draft. The review process took me and Dr. Chen several months to complete. With the cooperation of all authors, we completed the process by the end of December 2015, a record time, according to the staff of the press. The book ended with eighty authors and 454 pages. The months of January and February of 2016 were slow time for the Press due to the Lunar New Year holiday. The Press staff worked hard and was able to have the book printed in early February. The reason that we wanted it so was to try to distribute the book to the Chinese high-level officers when they had their major planning session of the Fifteenth Five-Year Plan in Beijing in early March of 2016. We printed 5,000 softcover books and 150 hardcover books. The hardcover books were not available for sale. It was for Dr. Chen and I to use as a special gift to important people. My good friend Mr. Chen Zeming assisted us to distribute the books at the planning session. We also made the books available for sale at the Seventh International Forum of Food Safety in April of 2016. I purchased one thousand copies and distributed them to the library and the Agriculture Deans of every university and college in China with food safety or food quality program. Later, I was told that the book had a major influence on food safety guidelines of the food safety laws and regulation issued by the central and local government agencies.

After the Chinese book was published, a number of foreign scientists asked me whether we could consider translating the book into English. After some thought, Dr. Chen and I decided that we could do better than just translate the book into English. We could add more chapters and install global perspectives into the chapters in the Chinese book. Finally, the English book was entitled *Food Safety in China: Science, Technology, Regulation, and Management*. The book was published by Wiley-Blackwell of Oxford, UK, probably the best-known science book publisher in the world. For the English book, we added four new chapters and delete one chapter. For several chapters, new authors were added to provide a global perspective in addition to just the situation in China. In other words, the food safety situation in China was compared with the rest of the world, mostly to the Western countries of US, UK, Japan, Australia, and EU countries. The end result was that we had a book with 36 chapters, 101 authors, and 657 pages.

The collection of write-ups for the English books went exceptionally smooth. We had the idea for the English book in September 2016, and all chapter authors were confirmed in December 2016. By the end of June 2017, most of the chapters were completed. The editing of the chapters by the Wiley-Blackwell copy editors was very strict. The writing was in excellent English. Each chapter of the book was edited several times by me and the Wiley-Blackwell copy editors. The book was ready to be printed by December 2017. It officially became available for sale in January 2017. Wiley-Blackwell did not charge printing of the book, but we did have to pay for the editing, design, and marketing of the book. Dr. Chen and I decided that we would not take royalty of the book but use them to pay for cost of publishing the book, and Wiley-Blackwell agreed. I was very happy with the end product and learned a lot about the English language.

Overall, the two books took about two and a half years to complete, which was very fast by any standards. No one believed the speed of how fast the two books were done and available for sale. Naturally, we had a lot of assistance from the right person involved.

CHAPTER 27
World Travel

Travel was mostly a joy but sometimes it was a pain in the neck. Chasing luggage on a trip was no fun. One time, I went to Brazil for a conference at São Paulo. I made the tight connection at Miami, but my luggage did not. Since I had to visit three other cities in Brazil, one on each day, by local commuter flights, my luggage never caught up with me till the last day. I had to buy some clothes for daily activities.

By my last count, I had been to over seventy countries and territories of the world. Outside of Africa and Eastern Europe and South America, my footprints had covered many places of the world. I had been to all fifty states of the US and basically all provinces and autonomous regions in China. In particular, I had the opportunity to visit places not many tourists would go. I selected three of them to share with the readers.

One of the more interesting trips was to Oman, with Salina. We nearly missed the connection at London due to the three-plus hours of going through security and changing of terminals. However, once we arrived at Muscat, we were treated well. We were driven to a university town and stayed at Hilton Hotel. I was the lead member of the advisory committee in reviewing the programs of the Oman National University. The university had two campuses, one for male students and one for female students. The female students all wore masks and only had their eyes open to the outside. Originally, two other wives of the five members in the team would make the trip. After learning the strict rules of female behavior at Oman, they both backed out. The news was that a Dutch princess had a slipper on, and her ankle was shown. The airport security guide lached her bare ankle in public. Salina decided that it was probably the only chance in her life to visit an Arabian country, so she took the trip. Once we arrived at the university, they had to find ways to keep Salina company. They asked two expat foreign faculty wives, one from Malaysia and one from UK, to be her escort. While we were busy doing the review work every day, Salina was shown nearby tourist spots. The most memorable one was to go through a dried riverbed on a jeep, much like the *Indiana Jones* movie, as the scenery was very similar to that in the movie. Every evening at dinnertime, we would ask Salina to tell us about her day's visit, and everybody envied her good luck.

We had been to many places in China. Besides all the tourist spots, we visited Tibet, Xinjiang Uygur, and Ningxia Hui Autonomous Regions.

Tibet was declared as an autonomous region in 1965. The region was often closed to outside visitors. In fact, it was closed for two weeks before we took the trip and was closed two weeks after we took the trip. Thus, we were lucky to be able to visit the region. It was an exciting trip. Everyone who visited Tibet needed a visa permit and must have a Tibet tour guide as an escort. There was no individual freely traveling in the region. There were four of us who took the trip—me, Salina, and our best friends, Dr. Da-Lun Yang and Grace Lo Yang. To better adjust to the high altitude of the region, we took a special mountain train from Xining of Qinghai Province to reach Lhasa. The train was a twenty-four-hour ride, as it went through some of the tallest parts of China. We were told that more than seven hundred workers died during the construction of the railroad, and cold weather and strong winds caused the casualty. The construction started in 1984 and took over twenty years to complete and open for traffic on October 15, 2005. The train cabins were specially made to withstand the wind, and there were two locomotives, also specially made for the journey. The cabins were pressurized, and oxygen tank was available near the public restroom area. An extra bonus of the train ride was the view of the Kunlun Mountain Region from the windows. At one place, there were thirty mountaintops like the Fuji Mountain in Japan, one over another. There was no way to tell others how the feeling of personally viewing this picture.

When we arrived at the Lhasa train station, the security guard walked us to the exit where our tour guide was waiting for us. We were lucky that our tour guide was one of only four native Tibetans available in the whole region. We learned from him not only more insight information of the region but also about the culture of Tibetans and their religion. For example, the Tibetans had no family name. Once a person died, they would just leave the body in the wild for the hawks to eat the body. The tour guide was glad that we had good health, and we did not have any problem to the high altitude. He said that almost everyone who came to Lhasa would have problems. Vomiting two to four times per day was normal. Salina and I did take a special herb medicine for two weeks ahead of the time, and the medicine worked. The Yangs were used to the high altitude of Dillon, Colorado, where they had a second home, as they liked downhill skiing from nearby Vail, Colorado.

Our first stop of the visit was the Potala Palace, built in the seventh century. It was the tallest palace building in the world. The Tibet tourist bureau had a good way of controlling the number of tourists to be allowed in and out of the palace each hour. They made the tour guide responsible for getting their tour group members out of the palace within one hour. If not, they would fine the tour guide and cancel their license. We were lucky that with only the four of us, we were able to spend enough time to view the various tombs of the past lama and view a live worship session by the monks. One of the major problems with the palace was that there were no doors for any room. They used heavy cloth curtains as doors. For each room, there was a monk who would lift the curtain for the guest to enter or exit. The cloth curtains were filled with oil and smoke, which were used inside the rooms. We were not sure how often they were cleaned, if at all. The other thing the Tibet government did was to clear the houses used to be at or near the palace. It created a huge square almost the size of People's Square in Beijing. Tourists had plenty of space to take good photos of the palace in the background. That evening, we had a good Sichuan food meal and had a good night's sleep.

To me, the next day was the highlight of our trip. Tibet had two lamas. One lived in Lhasa, the other at Rikaze. Most tourists would take the highway to go from one to the other. We took the mountain road, which would pass the highest point of Tibet at over 5,000 meters. The twisting mountain roads took several hours to negotiate before we reached the highest point. There were no trees halfway up, and we saw many glaciers along the way. We came down from the car to touch the glaciers and had great photos taken. When we reached the highest point, Da-lun and Grace felt the attitude for the first and only time in Tibet. There was a beautiful lake, which was the Saint Lake of Tibet. No one was allowed to go nearby or touch the water. Strangely enough, there were no birds as well. We spent an hour there before driving for another two hours to reach the only small village town in the mountains with a two-star hotel for an overnight stay. The next day, we arrived at Rikaze and checked in the hotel. We had a good meal, and the tour guide led us to the local market, where the locals purchased their daily needs. We got many Tibetan handmade things for very reasonable prices.

The next day, we visited the Rikaze palace tombs and grounds. These tombs and grounds were small in scale in comparison with those in Lhasa. Nevertheless, each tomb had different designs. After lunch, we took the highway to return to Lhasa. Tibet had the best highway speed control system in the world. The total length of the trip was equal to two hundred miles. The speed limit was fifty miles per hour. At the beginning of the trip, the driver had to stop at the checking station to get a stamp and the time. After fifty miles, the driver had to check in the next station. If the car got to the station before an hour, it would be fined by the minute. The fine was quite high by Chinese standards. To avoid the fine, a couple of miles before we got to the next station, the driver would stop the car, and we would rest by the roadside till the time was up. Also, there was no public toilet facility, and we had to use the woods off the roadside to relieve ourselves. It took us more than four hours to return to Lhasa. We checked in at the same hotel for the overnight stay.

The next morning, we checked in at the airport and boarded the plane to Beijing and transferred to the US. That concluded our unique tour of Tibet.

Joseph and Salina visited Sydney Australia on January 22, 2020

I was invited by the Sichuan Agricultural University to give a presentation on their anniversary. The university was located at Yian, a small town south of Chengdu. Apparently, the Dean of Agriculture was at the International Forum on Food Safety and purchased my book. She met us at the Chengdu airport, and we drove for about two hours south to Yian. We checked in at an interesting hotel, which used to be the palace of a small tribal country, which was conquered by Tibet several hundred years ago. The hotel rooms were lined with panels made of Tibet tea bricks. It seemed that the tea bricks could adsorb odors and somehow kept the dust off the panels. Thus, the rooms had a slight tea smell, and we felt great. The other facilities were equal to a three-star hotel, and the food was not very good. After I finished my presentation and attended their event, the VP of the university hosted us at a unique eating place at the top of the hill where we could view the whole city, which was built around a river. We had a rare swordfish that was only available at one section of the river. The fish had a sword bone, which they put in a lovely box and presented to Salina. Salina needed some shoes and went to the local market and took two pairs for the price of less than one-third of the price for one pair in the US. They were good-quality shoes as well.

The next day, we drove to the city of Kongding. The newly opened highway was to have more tunnels than any highway in the world. They built two one-way roads. Salina had seen a photo of the highway taken by airplane. It was beautiful, with mountain sceneries. The architecture of the bridges between the tunnels was fantastic. However, when riding in the car, we did not see much of them. There were two stops that you had to walk down into the valley to take in some of the views. Also, some of the designs on the walls of the tunnel were lovely.

We reached Kongding in two-plus hours. Kongding was a small town with only one road in between the mountains on both sides. It was named after a folk song entitled "Kongding Love Song." Almost everyone in China knew how to sing the song.

There was a big stone carved with the song in the only square in town. We did see some foreign tourists there although it was packed with Chinese tourists. The town had a small commuter airport for small planes to Chengdu or Chongqing. We went to a good restaurant, spent two hours at some of the tourist spots, and returned to Yian before dark. The next day, we were taken to the Chengdu airport and boarded planes for the US.

With that, this marks the end of this book.

ABOUT THE AUTHOR

Joseph J. Jen was born at Chongqing, China, in 1939. He moved to the US in 1962 and lived there ever since. His life had many career changes: from academia professor to food industry executive, academia management, and Under-Secretary of the USDA. It is believed that he is the first and possibly only Asian American born in China who became a subcabinet appointee in the history of the US federal government. His life is full of interesting events, and he wrote the book in a story style rather than the traditional autobiography style. He has been an outstanding scientist, educator, and manager. He has many scientific publications and has received several high-profile awards. He and his wife of fifty-six years, Salina Fond Jen, lives in retirement at Las Vegas, Nevada, US. He has two children, Pauline and Jeffrey, and two grandchildren, Alexandra Jen Ryan and Colby Jen Ryan.

CPSIA information can be obtained
at www.ICGtesting.com
Printed in the USA
LVHW060101200721
693164LV00003B/229